ETHOS: Individual, Social, Cultural, Institutional

Copyright © Andreas Sofroniou, 2020.

ETHOS: Individual, Social, Cultural, Institutional

ISBN: **978-0-244-24961-8**

Copyright © Andreas Sofroniou, 2020.

ETHOS: Individual, Social, Cultural, Institutional

ISBN: **978-0-244-24961-8**

1

Andreas Sofroniou

Contents

Andreas Sofroniou

Ethos

The Greek word ēthos takes account of the character, sentiment, manners, moral nature, or guiding beliefs of a person, group, or institution and the predominant characteristics of a racial culture.

Disposition or character

In rhetoric, this is the speakers' or writer's character or emotions, articulated in the attempt to persuade an audience.

Ethos is also distinguished from pathos, which is the emotion the speaker or writer hopes to induce in the audience.

The two concepts were well known in a broader sense by ancient Classical authors, who used pathos when referring to the violent emotions and ethos to mean the calmer ones.

Ethos was the natural disposition or moral character, an abiding quality, and

4

pathos a temporary and often violent emotional state.

For Renaissance writers the distinction was a different one: ethos described character and pathos an emotional appeal.

Ethos diagram

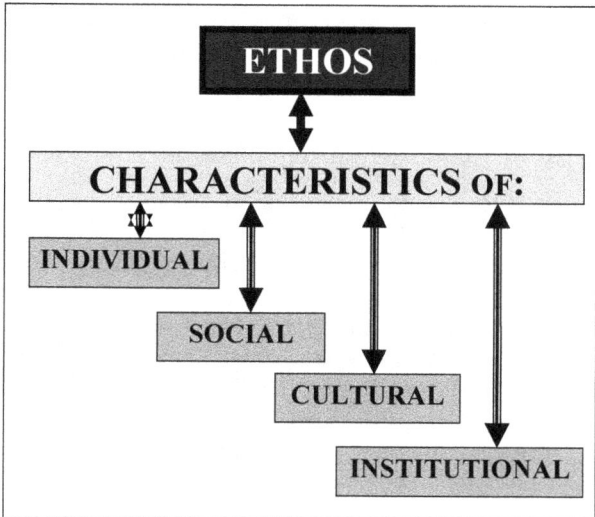

Ethology

On the other hand, ethology is the branch of science which investigates the development of systems of morals; now more generally, the science of human character.

Further on, ethology is the study of behaviour in a natural environment.

Ethology is particularly concerned with the animal's interactions with others of the same species and the function of the behaviour and is directed towards how the evolution of behaviour has been influenced by natural selection.

Its theoretical orientation was based on Darwin's dictum that patterns of behaviour as well as bodily structure are subject to the selective processes of evolution. Its classical formulation is in the works of the Austrian Konrad Lorenz (1903-89) and the Dutchman Nikolaas Tinbergen (1907-88), particularly the latter's The Study of Instinct (1951).

Tinbergen showed that complex patterns of behaviour might appear with little

6

influence of learning when innately programmed 'sign stimuli' release them. An example is the food-begging of herring gull chicks, which is 'released' by the orange spot on the adult bird's yellow beak.

Lorenz demonstrated how experience might direct a fixed action pattern when he discovered imprinting.

Goslings adopted him as their 'mother' because he was the first mobile object they encountered when newly hatched.

Lorenz and Tinbergen generally played down the role of learning, but in the 1950s and 1960s it became clear that animals' natural behaviour is more flexible, particularly in higher species such as primates.

Modern studies of animal behaviour nevertheless accept Tinbergen's view that any behaviour must be explained in four ways: its immediate cause; its appearance and progress in the development of the individual; its adaptive function--how it improves the

7

species' chance of survival; its evolutionary history--how the species developed such behaviour as part of its repertoire.

Ethology spread into systematic observation of human, particularly children's, behaviour, and arguments about innateness of facial expression and other non-verbal communication. Bowlby's theory of attachment is another application of ethological ideas.

Behaviour

Behaviour is the way an individual animal acts in response to its environment and to members of its own and other species.

The behaviour of an animal, just like its physiology or morphology, may be subject to the influence of natural selection, and may be important in providing survival value in many areas of an animal's life.

Behaviour can be inherited or learned. Even simple organisms show complex

8

inherited behaviour patterns: these are often referred to as instinctive behaviour.

They may facilitate feeding, as in the web-building of many spiders, or ensure successful reproduction, as in courtship behaviour. Inherited behaviour may provide communication between social animals, such as the waggle-dance of hive bees, which tells the closely related nest mates of the whereabouts of food.

Inherited behaviour patterns tend to be relatively inflexible and usually consist of a series of actions, each of which requires a particular signal or reaction from another individual.

More sophisticated organisms such as mammals also show inherited behaviour, for example when human infants cling instinctively to their mothers. In addition, the actions of many organisms are modified by experience, allowing an animal's behaviour to be better suited to a complex and changing environment.

Lion cubs, for example, learn to hunt by watching and copying their parents, whilst many insectivorous birds learn to avoid eating unpalatable prey through trial and error.

The well-developed brain of humans and other animals such as elephants, allows them to learn a wide range of complex behaviour patterns. These include complex social, manipulative, and mental skills, and in humans, speech.

Occasionally, learned behaviour patterns may be transmitted culturally from generation to generation, as with the novel food-washing behaviour of Japanese macaques.

The study of animal behaviour in the wild was transformed into a science by biologists such as Konrad Lorenz and Nikolaas Tinbergen, and is called ethology.

Ethologists attempt to understand, through observation and experiment, how behaviour in the natural environment has developed, how it works, and what its evolutionary significance is, particularly in terms of

10

the survival value that it provides for an animal under the influence of natural selection.

Learning

Learning is the process by which animals acquire knowledge about their environment and their relationship to it during their own lifetime.

Learning is thought to occur when, as a result of experience, connections in the brain are made which allow an animal to form an association between events in the world around it: either between an event and a consequence of it which affects the animal, or between an action and an event.

Learning is therefore inferred to have taken place when an animal changes its behaviour in response to previous experience. Learning has been demonstrated in animals ranging from protozoa to humans, and may involve anything from very simple learned responses such as aversion to noxious stimuli, to the very complex learning of speech in humans.

Learning is generally taken to include a variety of long-term changes. For example, learning may occur as a result of reinforcement either through reward or through punishment. In classical (Pavlovian) conditioning, the arrival of a rewarding food pellet follows a short time after the presentation of a stimulus, such as light or tone, and the animal quickly learns to associate the stimulus with the arrival of the food pellet.

Ultimately, the conditioned stimulus, the light or tone, may itself cause behaviour normally associated with feeding, such as salivation. In instrumental (operant) conditioning, it is the animal's own actions that trigger the arrival of the reward.

This type of conditioning may teach a rat to press a bar in order to obtain food, or to avoid a punishing electric shock. Similarly, in the wild, the blue tit may learn to rip open the foil tops of milk

12

bottles in order to obtain a nourishing drink.

Not all learning, however, appears to involve such obvious relationships between stimulus and reward. Young birds, for example, may go through a sensitive period during development in which they learn the characteristics of their species' typical song, or the appearance of members of the opposite sex, a process known as imprinting.

Although there is still considerable debate concerning the degree to which the fundamental processes of learning are specialized in different species, or whether different species simply employ similar processes to do different tasks, the end result is an enormous variety in the capacities of animals to learn different things.

Food-storing birds, for example, have an enlarged region of the brain known as the hippocampus, thought to be important in spatial memory, and can learn and recall the locations of hundreds of individually stored seeds.

13

Rats, which are highly dependent on tastes and odours because of their poor eyesight, and which feed in meals, are capable of associating illness with eating a new type of food, even if the effects only occur many hours later.

Social learning

The social learning theory is an adaptation of principles of learning to explain aspects of personality and behaviour.

In Social Learning and Imitation (1941) and other works, the US psychologists John Dollard and Neal Miller explained phenomena described by Freud as the products of mechanisms outlined by their behaviourist colleague Clark Hull (1884-1952).

They held that complex repertoires of behaviour are developed through reward and punishment ('reinforcement'). They applied their ideas to neurosis and its cure, but are now best known for their

14

theory that aggression results from the frustration of goal-directed behaviour.

Later, in a series of books such as Aggression (1973) and Social Foundations of Thought and Language (1985), the Canadian psychologist Albert Bandura paid particular attention to children's capacity for imitation and ability to learn by abstracting rules from their observation of others' performances, showing that such learning occurs without reinforcement.

Modern social learning theory emphasizes cognitive rather than motivational factors, and the roles of curiosity and the individual's belief in his or her ability to act effectively.

Imprinting

Imprinting is a process of early learning by which the new-born forms attachment to the object it sees first after birth.

It was made famous by the Austrian pioneer in ethology, Konrad Lorenz

15

(1903-89), who described it in Studies on Animal and Human Behaviour (1935). Recently hatched swimming and walking birds, such as ducklings, follow almost any noticeable moving object, normally their mother, thereby improving their chances of survival.

Such 'filial imprinting' is attachment to an individual care-giver. 'Sexual imprinting' is preference for the species of that same individual in later mate selection. Imprinting is a form of learning which requires no reward.

Indeed, the more effort the young has to exert to follow, the stronger the imprinting is. It shows how instinct interacts with circumstance in the development of behaviour and how important early experience may be.

Locus of control

Loci of control is a theory about the places (locus) people believe is the seat of control over their lives: 'internals' believe control is in their own hands,

16

'externals' believe in luck or other people's power over them.

The US psychologist Julian Rotter (1899-) proposed a social learning theory model of personality development, in which control beliefs underlie many differences of personality and motivation between people. His questionnaire to tap people's control beliefs, published in 1966, has been used world-wide.

Research has borne out many of Rotter's claims, showing that internality is associated with political activism and general eagerness to control one's surroundings, while externality is associated with depression and inability to cope with stress.

However, doubts have been expressed about whether people have general beliefs about their control and about the universality of the range of topics in Rotter's questionnaire.

Learned helplessness

This is a theory of depression formulated by the US psychologist Martin Seligman in his book Helplessness (1975) and later developed into an attributional theory.

Learned helplessness occurs in response to prolonged or repeated inescapable punishment of some sort, the key symptom being a passive, listless, or defeatist response to simple problems.

Bad events are believed to be caused by factors--such as stupidity, or weakness of will--which are 'internal' (an aspect of oneself), 'stable' (will remain), and 'global' (affect other areas of one's life).

Good events in contrast are believed to have external, transient, and specific causes, such as momentary good luck. The concept is therefore related to other locus of control theories. Psychotherapy may provide effective treatment.

18

Communication

Communication is the mutual exchange of information between individuals, a process central to human experience and social organization. The study of communication involves many disciplines, including linguistics, psychology, sociology, and anthropology.

All forms of communication, from interpersonal to mass media communications, involve an initiator, who formulates a message and sends it as a signal, by means of a particular channel, to a receiver, who decodes and interprets the meaning. In interpersonal communication involving face-to-face conversation, communication is direct, using the code of language, and reinforced by non-verbal communication such as body movement, eye contact, gesture, and facial expression. Response is also direct. Interpersonal communication can also take place at a distance.

19

Other forms of communication use writing and printing as the means of conveying messages. The invention of the printing press was the first step in the development of mass communication.

Books, newspapers, and periodicals are able to convey messages to a wide audience; an even wider audience is reached by radio and television, film, and the recording industries.

The mass media and the arts impose their own codes and characteristics on to their messages, which can range from relatively straightforward ideological tracts to complex texts carrying multiple layers of possible meaning.

Attachment

Attachment (in psychology) is the bonding of an infant with his or her caregiver. Investigations of attachment have been one of the major achievements of child psychology since World War II.

The UK child psychiatrist John Bowlby (1907-90) was one of the pioneers, preparing in 1951 an influential study Material Care and Mental Health for the World Health Organization, which was alarmed by the plight of the multitude of children orphaned or separated from their families.

Research has shown that the infants' successful development and maintenance of a bond with a specific person is necessary for healthy emotional, social, and personality growth.

The bond usually develops in the child's second six months and seems to be related to the intensity of the interaction rather than simply to the time spent together.

The child often has several attachments, but the most important is usually with the mother, although it may be with the father, siblings, or someone else.

What is particularly damaging for a child is if he or she is never able to form attachments (for example, because of placement in an orphanage with transient caregivers) or if attachments are repeatedly broken (for example, because of moves between a series of temporary foster homes).

Although the damage can sometimes be repaired if the child is later able to form a strong attachment to an adult, many such children grow up to be lacking in self-esteem, to be aggressive, delinquent, or subject to depression and unable themselves to form attachments. Bowlby's main work was the three-volume Attachment and Loss (1969-80), in which he explored attachment behaviour and its significance for adults and for children growing up in families as well as for separated children.

Natural selection

Natural selection is the process of differential survival and reproduction that enables evolution to take place.

22

The concept was invented by Darwin, and is the accepted explanation both of evolution and of the fact that organisms are well designed for living in their natural surroundings.

The argument is as follows. Organisms produce more offspring than can survive. Thus, there will be competition for survival. Only those organisms that are well designed for survival will live to reproduce.

If the properties that enabled them to survive are inherited, then the organisms of the next generation will resemble the successful members of the previous generation. Thus, the organisms best fitted for survival are selected by nature for reproduction.

As environments change, so also do the factors that make one individual better 'fitted' than another to reproduce. The constant selection, or survival of the 'fittest', is the eternal force that drives evolution.

Natural selection has been confirmed by observation, and studied by experiment. In a population of peppered moths, Biston betularia, for example, of which some were better camouflaged than others, birds have been seen to eat more of the poorly camouflaged type.

This results in evolution towards an increase in the proportion of better-camouflaged moths. The agent of natural selection, in this example, is visual hunting by birds. Even a very slight advantage of one individual over another is sufficient to cause changes in the population.

Evolution

Evolution (in biology) is the theory that all animal and plant species are related by common ancestry. It provides the unifying basis of all biological science.

The history of life is a single process of species-splitting and change. Evidence of evolution is found in the distribution of structures considered to be homologous:

24

structures which share the same developmental (embryonic) origin, and perhaps the same relative position, in different species (for example, the wing of a bird, the fore-leg of a dog, a human arm). Homologies can now be identified at the molecular and genetic level of an organism's composition.

A hierarchical Linnaean classification can be constructed by studying such similarities and differences.

Charles Darwin recognized the significance of this natural hierarchy (as had earlier naturalists, such as Lamarck), and argued that it arose from the actual genealogical relationship of organisms. Darwin (and A. R. Wallace) provided a causal evolutionary mechanism: natural selection.

Many different lines of evidence contribute to current evolutionary theory: genetics provides the scientific basis for the study of heredity and mutation; biogeography supplies evidence of geographical variation within and between species (Galapagos finches are

25

a good example of this variation); palaeontology and geology have revealed the time-span of the history of life on earth (over 3,500 million years), and the sequence of origination of the major groups of organisms.

Evolution as a historical event is now accepted widely as fact, but theories of evolutionary processes continue to be the subject of intense debate.

Natural selection leading to the increased adaptation of an organism may be significant only in the short-term of geological time, which encompasses numerous mass-extinction events.

The Darwinian model of gradual evolutionary change has been complemented by the theory of short bursts of rapid change which punctuate long periods of evolutionary stasis.

Geneticists and developmental biologists are researching the potential of large scale mutations, and possible constraints on the evolving structure of organisms.

Facial expression

Facial expression is an important form of non-verbal communication between individual humans.

Darwin argued that facial and other expressive actions are innate. He cited evidence of the universality of human expressions and of similarities between them and the expressions of other mammals, especially other primates.

In contrast, 20th-century anthropologists have described the enormous variation in the expressive behaviour of different cultures. Recent work supports a modified Darwinian view.

The basic facial expressions of happiness and sadness seem to be universal and the expressions of disgust, anger, fear, and surprise almost so.

These six expressions appear very early in blind or brain-damaged as well as normal infants, and are therefore unlikely to be learnt. But different cultures have different rules about the appropriateness of displaying particular emotions.

27

Two different nerve pathways control facial muscles, one is from the cortex, the brain's highly developed outer layer, which is responsible for our learning ability, and the other from lower brain centres, which control emotion. This explains how facial expressions can be innate and associated with particular emotions, but also come under subsequent control through social learning.

Ethology and animal behaviour

This is the study of animal behaviour. Although many naturalists have studied aspects of animal behaviour through the centuries, the modern science of ethology is usually considered to have arisen as a discrete discipline with the work in the 1920s of biologists Nikolaas Tinbergen of the Netherlands and Konrad Lorenz of Austria.

Ethology is a combination of laboratory and field science, with strong ties to certain other disciplines—e.g., neuroanatomy, ecology, evolution. The ethologist is interested in the behavioural process rather than in a particular animal group and often studies one type of behaviour (e.g., aggression) in a number of unrelated animals.

Ethologists

Ethologists start with the persuasive argument that study of animal warfare may contribute toward an understanding of war as employed by man. The behaviour of monkeys and apes in captivity and the behaviour of young children, for example, show basic similarities. In both cases, it is possible to observe that aggressive behaviour usually arises from several drives: rivalry for possession, the intrusion of a stranger, or frustration of an activity.

The major conflict situations leading to aggression among animals, especially those concerning access of males to females and control of a territory for feeding and breeding, are usually associated with patterns of dominance.

The analogies of animal to human behaviour drawn by many ethologists, however, are severely questioned by their more restrained colleagues as well as by many social scientists. The term "aggression," for example, is imprecisely and inconsistently used, often referring merely to the largely symbolic behaviour of animals involving such signals as grimaces.

Observed animal behaviour can be regarded as a possible important source of inspiration for hypotheses, but these must then be checked through the study of actual human behaviour. As this has not yet been adequately done, the hypotheses advanced have little foundation and are merely interesting ideas to be investigated.

Further, human behaviour is not fixed to the extent that animal behaviour is, partly because man rapidly evolves different patterns of behaviour in response to environmental factors, such as geography, climate, and contact with other social groups. The variety of these behaviour patterns is such that they can be used on both sides of an argument concerning, for example, whether or not men have an innate tendency to be aggressive.

Two particularly interesting subjects studied by ethologists are the effects of overcrowding on animals and animal behaviour regarding territory. The study of overcrowding is incomplete, and the findings that normal behaviour patterns tend to break down in such conditions and that aggressive behaviour often becomes prominent are subject to the qualification that animal and human reactions to overcrowding may be different.

Ethologists have also advanced plausible hypotheses concerning biological means of population control through reduced fertility that occurs when animal populations increase beyond the capacity of their environment. Whether such biological control mechanisms

31

operate in human society, however, requires further investigation.

Overpopulation

This refers to an excess of people in relation to the resources available to sustain them. The UN's forecast of population growth suggests that between 1990 and 2025 the world's population will increase from 5.3 billion to 8.5 billion. Almost all of this increase will occur in the developing countries of Asia, Africa, and Latin America. By the late 1980s, 67 nations with 85 per cent of the developing world's population officially considered their growth rates too high.

The UN Population Fund now argues that environmental degradation is the gravest immediate threat posed by over-population, rather than shortages of food, fuel, and minerals as previously thought.

Overpopulation (together with excessive consumption by the developed world) is already contributing to desertification, loss of agricultural productivity through overuse of land, the destruction of forests and, through the increased burning of fossil fuels, the greenhouse effect.

Already many poor countries, especially in sub-Saharan Africa, are losing their ability to feed, shelter, and educate even their present populations, yet these are the very countries where population growth is expected to be highest.

The UN Population Fund believes that only development can stabilize the world's population and calls for sanitation, education, health care, and family planning in order to reduce fertility rates.

However, the youthful age structure of the world's population and the opposition of the Roman Catholic Church to family planning, especially in South America, mean that overpopulation is one of the severest challenges facing the planet.

Territorial imperative

Findings concerning the "territorial imperative" in animals—that is, the demarcation and defence against intrusion of a fixed area for feeding and breeding—are even more subject to qualification when an analogy is drawn from them to human behaviour.

The analogy between an animal territory and a territorial state is obviously extremely tenuous. In nature the territories of members of a species differ in extent but usually seem to be provided with adequate resources, and use of force in their defence is rarely necessary, as the customary menacing signals generally lead to the withdrawal of potential rivals. This scarcely compares with the sometimes catastrophic defence of the territory of a national state.

Territory

Territory (in ecology) is the space defended by an organism or a group, using display or aggression, against others of the same species. It may be either temporary or permanent.

Many birds establish territories for nesting, as do some fishes, such as the stickleback. Male great tits, for example, set up breeding territories in the spring which provide an area in which to find food for the nestlings, and which are defended fiercely against any intruders not deterred by the resident's strenuous bouts of territorial bird song.

Territories may be large or small. A pride of lions may occupy territories several square kilometers in extent. The gannet in large breeding colonies maintains a territory of only about 1.5 m^2 (5 sq. feet), though in this case food is brought in from outside the territory. When the young of a species become mature, they are usually driven off to establish their own territories.

Territories usually only occur when some valuable resource, such as a feeding or nesting area, can be adequately defended. In some birds, such as the ruff, males may defend small territories on a

35

communal breeding ground, which they use solely to display to females.

Psychology

One school of theorists has postulated that the major causes of war can be found in man's psychological nature.

Such psychological approaches range from very general, often merely intuitive assertions regarding human nature to complex analyses utilizing the concepts and techniques of modern psychology. The former category includes a wide range of ethical and philosophical teaching and insights, including the works of such figures as St. Augustine and the 17th-century Dutch philosopher Spinoza.

Modern writers utilizing psychological approaches emphasize the significance of psychological maladjustments or complexes and of false, stereotyped images held by decision makers of other countries and their leaders. Some psychologists posit an innate

36

aggressiveness in man. Others concentrate upon public opinion and its influence, particularly in times of tension.

Others stress the importance of decision makers and the need for their careful selection and training. Most believe that an improved social adjustment of individuals would decrease frustration, insecurity, and fear and would reduce the likelihood of war.

All of them believe in the importance of research and education. Still, the limitations of such approaches derive from their very generality.

Also, whether the psychological premises are optimistic or pessimistic about the nature of man, one cannot ignore the impact upon human behaviour of social and political institutions that give man the opportunities to exercise his good or evil propensities and to impose restraints upon him.

Psychology is considered to be 'the science of mental life', in the words of James, one of its great figures.

Psychology concerns both the normal and abnormal workings of the mind, whereas psychiatry only deals with the latter.

The earliest scientific psychology was the study in the 19th century of sensory perception. This and other major psychological problems were defined earlier by the philosophers Locke and Hume, who theorized about emotion, motivation, sensation, memory, and understanding.

The first psychology courses were established in the 1870s by Wundt at Leipzig and James at Harvard. Experimental method and the development of statistical tests have been crucial to psychology's advance.

But major discoveries have been made through more informal work, such as the conversational studies of children's reasoning by Piaget. In Austria, Freud created psychoanalysis in the course of treating neurosis, but turned it into a general theory of personality, motivation, child development, and mental illness.

A recurrent question in behaviour genetics is the relative impact of heredity and experience, particularly very early experience. Galton introduced modern methods for investigating this, still a dominant issue in studies of sex differences and of intelligence and personality.

Progress in mid-20th-century psychology centred on learning theories, especially those of behaviourism, associated with Watson, and Skinner. These derived general laws of learning from animal experiments on the control of behaviour through conditioning. This work has had important applications in clinical psychology and the treatment of psychiatric illness.

However, in the 1950s behaviourism's oversimplified conceptual base and sacrifice of realism to experimental rigour came to seem increasingly inadequate. This was one reason for the rise of humanistic psychology.

Technological advances are helping to overcome these problems: it is now possible to record the activities of the brain in various ways; knowledge of genetics has increased dramatically; and computers assist in statistical analysis.

Computers have also provided a reference point for cognitive psychology, which since World War II has become the dominant area of research. It grew out of work on memory and problem-solving, and from the analogy with computers. It concerns itself with just those kinds of questions for which behaviourism appeared manifestly inadequate: language development, and the nature and development of human thought and knowledge.

Cognitive psychology shares its ancestry in German Gestalt psychology with modern social psychology, the other major development since World War II. Social psychology addresses such topics as prejudice, relationships, and misunderstandings of ourselves and others.

It has also been influenced by ethology.

Psychology finds application in industry, advertising, education, child-rearing, and, through clinical psychology, in the diagnosis and treatment of psychiatric illness.

Adjustment policies

Adjustment, in economics, is a term used to cover policies to adjust the economy to shocks, caused, for example, by sharp changes in commodity prices, and to promote efficiency and growth.

Adjustment policies usually include stabilization policies, which are directed at reducing imbalances in a country's economy, particularly deficits in its balance of payments, usually by promoting exports, reducing imports, increasing government revenue, and cutting public expenditure.

Adjustment policies supported by the World Bank also provide for a greater role for the market, with measures such as reduced price controls, privatization, encouragement of foreign investment, and import liberalization.

In the 1980s, world recession, falling commodity prices, and a large debt burden compelled many developing countries, especially in Latin America and Africa, to undertake stabilization and adjustment policies under the auspices of the IMF and the World Bank.

Amended versions of such policies are being implemented in the republics of the former Soviet Union and former Eastern bloc in the switch from planned to free market economies. Adjustment policies may be slow to take effect, depending in particular on adequate levels of investment, and are likely to cause hardship as unemployment rises, subsidies are cut, and government spending on social services is reduced.

In Adjustment with a Human Face (1987), UNICEF called for modified policies to avert such hardship, by maintaining output and investment, creating opportunities for small farmers and the urban poor, reallocating government

42

spending from high-cost areas such as hospitals to low-cost basic services such as clinics, and introducing public-works schemes to generate employment.

Social theories of war

Whereas psychological explanations of war contain much that seems to be valid, they are insufficient because man behaves differently in different social contexts.

Hence, many thinkers have sought their explanations in these contexts, focusing either on the internal organization of states or on the international system within which these operate.

The most voluminous and influential theories attributing war to the nature of the state fall into two broad streams, which can be loosely called liberal and socialist.

43

Social structure and interrelationships

Social structure, a term used by sociologists to refer to the discernible pattern of interrelationships in a society, which endure over time.

The social structure of a society is often held either to influence or to determine the experience of its members.

Thus, in a racially segregated society, the poverty of one race and the wealth of another may be explained not by the inherent characteristics of the two groups, but by the social structure.

In such a society, the operation and interrelationship of, for example, legal, political, and educational institutions can be shown to favour one group at the expense of the other.

Liberal analyses

The early or classical liberals of the 18th and 19th centuries distinguished three basic elements in their analysis—individuals, society, and the state—and regarded the state as the outcome of the interaction of the former two.

They assumed that society is self-regulating and that the socioeconomic system is able to run smoothly with little interference from the government.

Economy, decentralization, and freedom from governmental control were the classical liberal's main concerns, as shown particularly clearly in the writings of John Stuart Mill.

They accepted the necessity of maintaining defence but postulated the existence of a basic harmony of interests among states, which would minimize the incidence of wars.

Economic cooperation based upon an international division of labour and upon free trade would be in the interests of everybody—commerce would be the great panacea, the rational substitute for war.

In explanation of wars that did occur, however, liberals emphasized a variety of factors. First, they focused on autocratic governments, which were presumed to wage war against the wishes of peacefully inclined people.

It thus became a major tenet of liberal political philosophy that war could be eliminated by introducing universal suffrage because the people would surely vote out of office any belligerently inclined government.

From the early American pamphleteer Thomas Paine onward, a major school of liberals supported republicanism and stressed the peaceful impact of public opinion.

Although they could not agree about actual policies, they stressed certain general ideas concerning relations between states, paralleling their laissez-faire ideas.

Also, of the internal organization of the state with ideas of a minimum amount of international organization, use of force strictly limited to repelling aggression, the importance of public opinion and of democratically elected governments, and

46

rational resolution of conflicts and disputes.

Later in the course of the 19th century, however, and especially after World War I, liberals began to accept the conclusion that an unregulated international society did not automatically tend toward peace and advocated international organization as a corrective.

Liberalism

Liberalism is a political outlook attaching supreme importance to safeguarding the freedom of the individual within society. Liberal ideas first took shape in the struggle for religious toleration in the 16th and 17th centuries.

The liberal view was that religion was a private matter; it was not the business of the state to enforce a particular creed.

This later developed into a more general doctrine of the limited and constitutional state, whose boundaries were set by the natural rights of the individual (for

47

instance in the political thought of Locke).

Around 1800 liberalism became associated with the doctrines of the free market and laissez-faire, and reducing the role of the state in the economic sphere.

This tendency was reversed later in the 19th century with the arrival of 'New Liberalism', committed to social reform and welfare legislation. In contemporary debate both schools of thought are represented, some liberals harking back to the classical economic ideas of the late 18th century (for instance, Hayek), others embracing the mixed economy and the welfare state (for instance, Rawls).

Despite their economic disagreements, liberals unite in upholding the importance of personal liberty in the face of encroachment by the state, leading to demands for constitutional government, civil rights, and the protection of privacy.

Women voting

Known as suffragists, this British militant feminist movement campaigned for the right of adult British women to vote in general elections.

The Women's Social and Political Union, which was founded by Emmeline Pankhurst in 1903, gained rapid support, using as its weapons attacks on property, demonstrations, and refusal to pay taxes. There was strong opposition to giving women the vote at national level, partly from calculations of the electoral consequences of enfranchising women.

Frustration over the defeat of Parliamentary bills to extend the vote led the suffragettes to adopt militant methods to press their cause; Parliamentary debates were interrupted, imprisoned suffragettes went on strike, and one suffragette, flinging herself in front of the king's horse in the 1913 Derby horse-race, was killed.

These tactics were abandoned when Britain declared war on Germany in 1914 and the WSPU directed its efforts to support the war effort. In 1918, subject to educational and property qualifications, British women over 30 were given the vote (the age restriction was partly to avoid an excess of women in the electorate because of the deaths of men in the war). In 1928 women, over 21 gained the vote.

Socialism

Socialism refers to the political and economic theory of social organization, which advocates the conscious direction of social life, involving in particular limits on the private ownership of industry.

The word first appeared in France and Britain in the early 19th century in the writings of Saint-Simon and Fourier, and in Robert Owen's experiments at his New Lanark works in co-operative control of industry. It covers a wide range of positions from communism at one extreme to social democracy at the other, and is therefore difficult to define with precision.

It is easier to say what socialists are for than what they are against, namely untrammelled capitalism, which in socialist eyes enriches the owners of capital at the expense of their employees, provides no security for the poor, and sacrifices the welfare of society to private gain.

Most socialists have responded by arguing that the community as a whole should own and control the means of production, distribution, and exchange to ensure a more equitable division of a nation's wealth, either in the form of state ownership of industry, or else in the form of ownership by the workers themselves.

They have also often advocated replacing the market economy by some kind of planned economy. The aim of these measures is to make industry socially responsible, and to bring about a much greater degree of equality in living standards. In addition, socialists have argued for special provision for those in need, in the form, for instance, of a welfare state.

Socialism as a political ideal was revolutionized by Karl Marx in the mid-19th century, who tried to demonstrate scientifically how capitalist profit was derived from the exploitation of the worker, and argued that a socialist society could be achieved only by a mass movement of the workers themselves.

Both the methods by which this transformation was to be achieved and the manner in which the new society was to be run remained the subject of considerable disagreement and produced a wide variety of socialist parties, ranging from moderate reformers to ultra left-wing communists dedicated to upheaval by violent revolution.

A revolutionary upheaval is represented by Marx and Engels in The Communist Manifesto (1848) as necessary in order to replace capitalism. Bernstein (see revisionism) in Evolutionary Socialism

52

(1898) states that capitalism can be modified and changed by gradual, parliamentary methods.

These debates have been somewhat overshadowed in recent years by the question of whether socialism is viable at all as an alternative to capitalism. Most Western socialists now opt for social democracy, others for market socialism. It is only in certain developing countries that traditional socialist aims still attract widespread support among political leaders.

Socialist analyses

Whereas liberals concentrated on political structures, regarding them as of primary importance in determining the propensity of states to engage in war, socialists turned to the socioeconomic system of states as the primary factor.

Early in the 20th century the two streams did to some extent converge, as evidenced by the fact that the English

53

radical liberal John Hobson explained wars in terms later adopted by Lenin.

Karl Marx attributed war not to the behaviour of states but to the class structure of society. To him wars occurred not as an often voluntary instrument of state policy but as the result of a clash of social forces.

To Marx the state was merely a political superstructure; the primary, determining factor lies in the capitalist mode of production, which leads to the development of two antagonistic classes: the bourgeoisie and the proletariat. The bourgeoisie controls governmental machinery in its own interests.

In its international relations, the capitalist state engages in wars because it is driven by the dynamism of its system— the constantly growing need for raw materials, markets, and supplies of cheap labour. The only way to avoid war is to remove its basic cause, by replacing capitalism with socialism, thus abolishing both class struggle and states.

The Marxist doctrine, however, gave no clear guidance about the interim period before the millennium is reached; and the international solidarity of the proletariat proved a myth when war broke out in 1914, facing the European Social Democratic parties with the problem of adopting an attitude to the outbreak of the war.

The Second International of working-class parties had repeatedly passed resolutions urging the working classes to bring pressure upon their respective governments to prevent war, but, once war had broken out, each individual party chose to regard it as defensive for its own state and to participate in the war effort.

This was explained by Lenin as being due to a split in the organization of the proletariat that could be overcome only through the activity of a rigidly organized revolutionary vanguard.

Socialists in the West turned increasingly, although in varying degrees, to revisionist interpretations of

Marxism and returned to their attempts to revise socioeconomic structures through evolutionary constitutional processes, seeing this as the only possible means of preventing wars.

In the Soviet Union the socialist theory of war changed as the new communist regime responded to changes in circumstances. Soviet theoreticians distinguished three major types of war: between capitalist states, between capitalist and socialist states, and colonial wars of liberation.

The internecine wars among capitalist states were supposed to arise from capitalist competition and imperialist rivalries, such as those that led to the two world wars. They were desirable, for they weakened the capitalist camp.

A war between capitalist and socialist states was one that clearly expressed the basic principle of class struggle and was, therefore, one for which the socialist states must prepare. Finally, wars of colonial liberation could be expected

56

between subjugated people and their colonial masters.

The weakness of the theory was that the two major expected types of war, the intra-capitalist and the capitalist-socialist, did not materialize as frequently as Soviet theoreticians had predicted. Further, the theory failed to adequately analyse the situation in the Soviet Union and in the socialist camp.

Even in communist countries, nationalism seems to have proved more powerful than socialism: "national liberation" movements appeared and had to be forcibly subdued in the Soviet Union, despite its communist regime.

In addition, war between socialist states was not unthinkable, as the doctrine indicated:

- Only the colossal preponderance of Soviet forces prevented a full-scale war in 1956 against Hungary and

- In 1968 against Czechoslovakia;

- **War between the Soviet Union and the People's Republic of China was a serious possibility for two decades after the Sino-Soviet split in 1962; and**

- **Armed conflict erupted between China and Vietnam after the latter country became the most powerful in Southeast Asia.**

Finally, the theory did not provide for wars of liberation against socialist states, such as that conducted by the Afghan mujahideen against the Soviet Union from 1979 to 1989.

Social class

Social class defines a division or order of society. Many observers have distinguished between the systems of social stratification found in pre-industrial societies, in which distinctions are primarily of rank and rest on long-established rights and duties and the systems found in industrialized societies, which are based on social class.

58

In The Communist Manifesto (1848) Marx identified classes in relation to the means of production. In capitalist societies, the dominant class, 'the bourgeoisie', owned the means of production, while 'the proletariat' laboured, their surplus production belonging not to themselves but to the bourgeoisie.

For Marx, the criterion of class was economic. Weber, who, with Marx, has strongly influenced 20th-century debate, defined the term more broadly to refer to an individual's ability to command resources: class position might be determined by skills as well as property. Weber also regarded status as a factor in social stratification.

Mid-20th-century sociologists took up the idea of status to the point where some, especially in the USA, denied the existence of clear economic class divisions in their country, while in communist states, classless societies were predicted.

However, evidence from across the world suggests that social class divisions based on occupation and economic standing are to be found in every society.

Class position is linked not only to command of private goods such as cars or household appliances, but also to access to resources such as health care, education, and housing.

Nationalism

Many theories claim or imply that wars result ultimately from the allegiance of men to nations and from the intimate connection between the nation and a state.

This link between the nation and the state is firmly established by the doctrine of national self-determination, which has become in the eyes of many the major basis of the legitimacy of states and the major factor in their establishment and break-up.

It was the principle on which the political boundaries of Eastern Europe and the Balkans were arranged after World War I and became the principal slogan of the anti-colonial movement of the 20th century, finding expression in Chapter I, article 1, of the Charter of the United Nations in the objective of "self-determination of peoples," as well as in the more specific provisions of Chapters XI and XII.

It is this intimate link between nationalism and statehood that renders them both so dangerous.

The rulers of a state are ultimately governed in their behaviour by what is loosely summed up as the "national interest," which occasionally clashes directly with the national interests of other states.

The ideal of the nation-state is never fully achieved. In no historical case does one find all members of a particular nation gathered within one state's boundaries.

Conversely, many states contain sizable national minorities. This lack of full correlation has frequently given rise to dangerous tensions that can ultimately lead to war.

A government inspired by nationalism may conduct a policy aiming at the assimilation of national minorities, as was the general tendency of central and eastern European governments in the interwar period; it may also attempt to reunite the members of the nation living outside its boundaries, as Adolf Hitler did.

National groups that are not in control of a state may feel dissatisfied with its regime and claim self-determination in a separate state, as demonstrated in the attempt to carve Biafra out of Nigeria and the separation of Bangladesh from Pakistan.

There is no rational basis for deciding on the extent to which the self-determination principle should be applied in allowing national minorities to break away.

As a rule, the majority group violently opposes the breakaway movement. Violent conflicts can ensue and, through foreign involvement, turn into international wars.

No suitable method has been found for divorcing nationalism from the state and for meeting national demands through adequate social and cultural provisions within a larger unit.

Such an attempt in the Austro-Hungarian Empire before its dissolution in World War I failed. Even the Soviet Union was not permanently successful in containing its large proportion of national minorities.

Nationalism not only induces wars but also, through the severity of its influence, makes compromise and acceptance of defeat more difficult. It thus tends to prolong the duration and increase the severity of wars.

Possibly, however, this is the characteristic only of new, immature nationalisms, for nationalism has ceased to be a major cause of conflict and war among the nations of Western Europe.

Nationalism is but one form of ideology: in all ages people seem to develop beliefs and try to proselytize others.

Even within particular ideological groups, schisms result in conflicts as violent as those between totally opposed creeds, and heretics are often regarded as more dangerous and hostile than opponents.

As long as individual states can identify themselves with explosive differences in beliefs, the probability of a war between states is increased, and its intensity is likely to be greater.

Modern interpretations

Discussing women and rhetoric, scholar Karlyn Kohrs Campbell notes that entering the public sphere was considered an act of moral transgression for females of the nineteenth century.

Creating an ethos within such restrictive moral codes, therefore, meant adhering to membership of what Nancy Fraser and

Michael Warner have theorised as 'counter-publics'.

Though feminist rhetorical theorists have begun to offer more nuanced ways to conceive of ethos, they remain cognisant of how these classical associations have shaped and still do shape women's use of the rhetorical tool.

Johanna Schmertz draws on Aristotelian ethos to re-interpret the term alongside feminist theories of subjectivity, writing that, "Instead of following a tradition that, it seems to me, reads ethos somewhat in the manner of an Aristotelian quality proper to the speaker's identity, a quality capable of being deployed as needed to fit a rhetorical situation.

Rhetorical scholar Michael Halloran has argued that the classical understanding of ethos "emphasises the conventional rather than the idiosyncratic, the public rather than the private".

Commenting further on the classical etymology and understanding of ethos, Halloran illuminates the interdependence between ethos and cultural context by arguing that "To have ethos is to manifest the virtues most valued by the culture too and for which one speaks".

While scholars do not all agree on the dominant sphere in which ethos may be crafted, some agree that ethos is formed through the negotiation between private experience and the public, rhetorical act of self-expression.

According to Nedra Reynolds, "ethos, like post-modern subjectivity, shifts and changes over time, across texts and around competing spaces".

However, Reynolds additionally discusses how one might clarify the meaning of ethos within rhetoric as expressing inherently communal roots.

In the era of mass-mediated communication, Oddo contends, one's ethos is often created by journalists and dispersed over multiple news texts. With this in mind, Oddo coins the term inter-textual ethos, the notion that a public figure's "ethos is constituted within and across a range of mass media voices" .

In "Black Women Writers and the Trouble with Ethos", scholar Coretta Pittman notes that race has been generally absent from theories of ethos construction and that this concept is troubling for black women.

Pittman writes, "Unfortunately, in the history of race relations in America, black Americans' ethos ranks low among other racial and ethnic groups in the United States.

More often than not, their moral characters have been associated with a criminalised and sexualised ethos in visual and print culture".

Character in Greek tragedy

The ways in which characters were constructed is important when considering ethos, or character, in Greek tragedy.

Augustus Taber Murray explains that the depiction of a character was limited by the circumstances under which Greek tragedies were presented.

These include the single unchanging scene, necessary use of the chorus, small number of characters limiting interaction, large outdoor theatres, and the use of masks, which all influenced characters to be more formal and simple.

Murray also declares that the inherent characteristics of Greek tragedies are important in the makeup of the characters.

One of these is the fact that tragedy characters were nearly always mythical characters. This limited the character, as well as the plot, to the already well-known myth from which the material of the play was taken.

The other characteristic is the relatively short length of most Greek plays. This limited the scope of the play and characterization so that the characters were defined by one overriding motivation toward a certain objective from the beginning of the play.

However, Murray clarifies that strict constancy is not always the rule in Greek tragedy characters. To support this, he points out the example of Antigone who, even though she strongly defies Creon at the beginning of the play, begins to doubt her cause and plead for mercy as she is led to her execution.

Several other aspects of the character element in ancient Greek tragedy are worth noting.

One of these, which C. Garton discusses, is the fact that either because of contradictory action or incomplete description, the character cannot be viewed as an individual, or the reader is left confused about the character.

One method of reconciling this would be to consider these characters to be flat, or type-cast, instead of round. This would mean that most of the information about the character centres around one main quality or viewpoint.

Comparable to the flat character option, the reader could also view the character as a symbol. Examples of this might be the Eumenides as vengeance, or Clytemnestra as symbolizing ancestral curse.

Yet another means of looking at character, according to Tycho von Wilamowitz and Howald, is the idea that characterization is not important. This idea is maintained by the theory that the play is meant to affect the viewer or reader scene by scene, with attention being only focused on the section at hand.

This point of view also holds that the different figures in a play are only characterized by the situation surrounding them, and only enough so that their actions can be understood.

Garet makes three more observations about a character in Greek tragedy:

1. The first is an abundant variety of types of characters in Greek tragedy.

2. His second observation is that the reader or viewer's need for characters to display a unified identity that is similar to human nature is usually fulfilled.

3. Thirdly, characters in tragedies include incongruities and idiosyncrasies.

Another aspect stated by Garet is that tragedy plays are composed of language, character, and action, and the interactions of these three components; these are fused together throughout the play. He explains that action normally determines the major means of characterisation.

71

Another principle he states is the importance of these three components' effect on each other; the important repercussion of this being character's impact on action.

Augustus Taber Murray also examines the importance and degree of interaction between plot and character. He does this by discussing Aristotle's statements about plot and character in his Poetics: that plot can exist without character, but the character cannot exist without plot, and so the character is secondary to the plot.

Murray maintains that Aristotle did not mean that complicated plot should hold the highest place in a tragedy play.

This is because the plot was, more often than not, simple and therefore not a major point of tragic interest. Murray conjectures that people today do not accept Aristotle's statement about character and plot because to modern people, the most memorable things about tragedy plays are often the characters.

Character, or ethos, in pictorial narrative

Ethos, or character, also appears in the visual art of famous or mythological ancient Greek events in murals, on pottery, and sculpture referred to generally as pictorial narrative.

Aristotle even praised the ancient Greek painter Polygnotos because his paintings included characterization. The way in which the subject and his actions are portrayed in visual art can convey the subject's ethical character and through this the work's overall theme, just as effectively as poetry or drama can.

This characterisation portrayed men as they ought to be, which is the same as Aristotle's idea of what ethos or character should be in tragedy.

Accordingly, this was the reason for the representation of character, or ethos, in public paintings and sculptures. In order to portray the character's choice, the pictorial narrative often shows an earlier scene than when the action was committed.

73

Stansbury-O'Donnell gives an example of this in the form of a picture by the ancient Greek artist Exekia which shows the Greek hero Ajax planting his sword in the ground in preparation to commit suicide, instead of the actual suicide scene.

Additionally, Castriota explains that ancient Greek art expresses the idea that character was the major factor influencing the outcome of the Greeks' conflicts against their enemies. Because of this, "ethos was the essential variable in the equation or analogy between myth and actuality".

Ideology

Ideology is a political belief-system that explains the world as it currently is and suggests how it should be changed.

The term was given currency by Marx, who used it to describe the belief-systems of social classes, and especially that of the capitalist class or bourgeoisie.

Bourgeois ideology involved false consciousness, and in that respect was contrasted with the 'scientific' outlook that represented the true consciousness of the working class.

This ideology/science contrast has since generally been dropped in favour of the view that all political outlooks rest on assumptions that cannot be proved, and are to that degree ideological.

Some have sought to reserve the term for political outlooks that are seen as rigid and extreme in contrast to those that are more pragmatic and moderate. In this sense, social scientists in the 1950s and 1960s, such as Edward Shils and Daniel Bell, claimed that Western societies were witnessing 'the end of ideology', pointing especially to the demise of Marxism as an all-embracing vision of society.

It seems better, however, to recognize the pervasiveness of ideology as the means by which people order their perceptions of the social world, whether or not they consciously subscribe to a political creed.

National demand

This is the term for the demand made by members of a nation for political self-government, which normally entails the founding of an independent state.

Nations are very hard to define, but roughly speaking they are bodies of people who identify with one another and acknowledge a common loyalty by virtue of descent, language, culture, or religion.

Such national identities have proved remarkably resilient in the modern world, and they have been a potent source of political change.

Early nationalist movements, such as those in Germany and Italy in the 19th century, were typically concerned to build large and powerful states out of existing small principalities.

In the present century nationalists have more often sought either to throw off imperial or colonial rule (many developing countries have witnessed nationalist movements aiming at the formation of independent states) or else to break away from an established state.

Recent European movements, such as those of the Scots, the Basques, and the many minorities or nationalities within the erstwhile Soviet Union, show nationalism taking this secessionist form.

Fierce fighting occurred in Georgia, Armenia, Azerbaijan, and Moldova as different groups sought to establish separate nations for themselves.

Liberals and socialists have often been inclined to dismiss nationalism as an irrational phenomenon arising from the most primitive elements in human nature, but few would now deny the mobilizing power of national sentiments and allegiances.

Special-interest groups

Whereas some theories of war regard the state as an undifferentiated whole and generalize about its behaviour, other

77

theorists are more sociologically oriented and focus on the roles played within the state by various special-interest groups.

A distinction is made by these theorists between the great mass of people and those groupings directly involved, or influential with government.

The people, about whose attitudes adequate knowledge is lacking, are generally assumed to be taken up with their daily lives and to be in favour of peace.

The influential groups, who are directly involved in external affairs and, hence, in wars, are the main subject of analysis.

A Warlike government dragging peace-loving people into international conflict is a recurrent theme of both liberal and socialist analyses of war.

Some writers have gone to the length of postulating a continuous conspiracy of the rulers against the ruled that can be traced to prehistoric times, when priests and warriors combined in the first state structures.

78

Most writers, however, narrow the field and seek an answer to the question of why some governments are more prone to engage in war than others are, and they generally find the answer in the influence of important interest groups that pursue particular and selfish ends.

The chief and most obvious of such groups is the military. Military prowess was a major qualification for political leadership in primitive societies; the search for military glory as well as for the spoils of victory seems to have been one of the major motivations for war.

Once the military function became differentiated and separated from civilian ones, a tension between the two became one of the most important issues of politics.

The plausible view has generally been held that the military strive for war, in which they attain greater resources and can satisfy their status seeking and, sometimes, also an aspiration for direct and full political power.

79

In peacetime, the military are obviously less important, are denied resources, and are less likely to influence or attain political power directly.

At the same time, a second, although usually subsidiary, consideration of the military as a causal agent in war holds that an officer corps is directly responsible for any fighting and is thus more aware of its potential dangers for its members and for the state as well.

Although intent on keeping the state in a high state of preparedness, the military may be more cautious than civilians about engaging in war. It is often held, however, that increased military preparedness may result in increased tensions and thus indirectly lead to the outbreak of war.

Closely allied are theories about groups that profit from wars economically—capitalists and the financiers, especially those involved in industries catering to war.

All this play a central part as the villains of the piece in socialist and liberal theories of war, and even those not subscribing to such theories do not deny the importance of military-industrial complexes in countries in which large sectors of the economy specialize in war supplies.

But, although industrialists in all the technologically advanced systems are undoubtedly influential in determining such factors as the level of armaments to be maintained, it is difficult to assume that their influence is or could be decisive when actual questions concerning war or peace are being decided by politicians.

Finally, some scientists and technologists constitute a new, much smaller, but important group with special interests in war.

To some extent one can generalize about them, although the group is heterogeneous, embracing as it does nuclear scientists, space researchers, biologists and geneticists, chemists, and engineers.

If they are involved in defence work, they all share the interest of the military in securing more resources for their research: without their military applications, for example, neither nuclear nor space research would have gone ahead nearly as fast as it has.

War, however, does not enhance the status and standing of scientists; on the contrary, they come under the close control of the military.

They also usually have peaceful alternatives to military research, although these may not be very satisfactory or ample.

Consequently, although modern war technology depends heavily upon scientists and although governments in work directly or indirectly concerned with this technology employ many of them, scientists as a group are far from being wedded to war.

On the contrary, many of them are deeply concerned with the mass destruction made possible by science and participate in international pacifist movements.

Ethos meaning character

In this case, Ethos meaning "character" is used to describe the guiding ideals that characterises a community, nation, or ideology.

The classical Hellenes also used this word to refer to the power of music to influence emotions, and behavioural patterns.

Modern usage of the term

In modern usage, ethos denotes the disposition, character, or fundamental values peculiar to a specific person, people, corporation, culture, or movement.

Ethos therefore may change in response to new ideas or forces. Aristotle, however, broadens the concept to include expertise and knowledge. Ethos is limited, in his view, by what the speaker says.

Others, however, contend that a speaker's ethos extends to the overall moral character and history of the speaker. That is, what people think of his or her character before the speech has even begun.

END

Index   *Page*

Andreas Sofroniou

Andreas Sofroniou

Bibliography

ALL BOOKS LISTED BELOW ARE PUBLISHED BY ANDREAS SOFRONIOU

1. THERAPEUTIC PSYCHOLOGY, ISBN: 978-1-326-34523-5
2. MEDICAL ETHICS THROUGH THE AGES, ISBN: 978-1-4092- 7468-1
3. MEDICAL ETHICS, FROM HIPPOCRATES TO THE 21ST CENTURY ISBN: 978-1-4457-1203-1
4. MISINTERPRETATION OF SIGMUND FREUD, ISBN: 978-1-4467-1659-5
5. JUNG'S PSYCHOTHERAPY: THE PSYCHOLOGICAL & MYTHOLOGICAL METHODS, ISBN: 978-1-4477-4740-6
6. FREUDIAN ANALYSIS & JUNGIAN SYNTHESIS, ISBN: 978-1-4477-5996-6
7. ADLER'S INDIVIDUAL PSYCHOLOGY AND RELATED METHODS, ISBN: 978-1-291-85951-5
8. ADLERIAN INDIVIDUALISM , JUNGIAN SYNTHESIS, FREUDIAN ANALYSIS, ISBN: 978-1-291-85937-9
9. PSYCHOTHERAPY, CONCEPTS OF TREATMENT, ISBN: 978-1-291-50178-0
10. PSYCHOLOGY, CONCEPTS OF BEHAVIOUR, ISBN: 978-1-291-47573-9
11. PHILOSOPHY FOR HUMAN BEHAVIOUR, ISBN: 978-1-291-12707-2
12. SEX, AN EXPLORATION OF SEXUALITY, EROS AND LOVE, ISBN: 978-1-291-56931-5
13. PSYCHOLOGY FROM CONCEPTION TO SENILITY, ISBN: 978-1-4092-7218-2
14. PSYCHOLOGY OF CHILD CULTURE, ISBN: 978-1-4092-7619-7
15. JOYFUL PARENTING, ISBN: 0 9527956 1 2
16. GUIDE TO A JOYFUL PARENTING, ISBN: 0 952 7956 1 2
17. THERAPEUTIC PHILOSOPHY FOR THE INDIVIDUAL AND THE STATE, ISBN: 978-1-4092-7586-2
18. PHILOSOPHIC COUNSELLING FOR PEOPLE AND THEIR GOVERNMENTS, ISBN: 978-1-4092-7400-1
19. CHILD PSYCHOTHERAPY, ISBN: 978-1-326-44169-2
20. HYPNOTHERAPY IN MEDICINE, PSYCHOLOGY, MAGIC, ISBN: 978-1-326-48163-6
21. ART FOR PSYCHOTHERAPY, ISBN: 978-1-326-78959-6
22. SLEEPING AND DREAMING EXPLAINED BY ARTS & SCIENCE, ISBN: ISBN: 978-1-326-81309-3
23. PHILOSOPHY AND POLITICS, ISBN: 978-1-326-33854-1
24. MORAL PHILOSOPHY, FROM SOCRATES TO THE 21ST AEON, ISBN: 978-1-4457-4618-0
25. MORAL PHILOSOPHY, FROM HIPPOCRATES TO THE 21ST AEON, ISBN: 978-1-84753-463-7
26. MORAL PHILOSOPHY, THE ETHICAL APPROACH THROUGH THE AGES, ISBN: 978-1-4092-7703-3
27. MORAL PHILOSOPHY, ISBN: 978-1-4478-5037-3
28. 2011 POLITICS, ORGANISATIONS, PSYCHOANALYSIS, POETRY, ISBN: 978-1-4467-2741-6
29. WISDOM AN ACCUMULATION OF KNOWLEDGE, ISBN: 978-1-326-99692-5
30. MYTHOLOGY LEGENDS FROM AROUND THE GLOBE, ISBN: 978-1-326-98630-8
31. PLATO'S EPISTEMOLOGY, ISBN: 978-1-4716-6584-4
32. ARISTOTLE'S AETIOLOGY, ISBN: 978-1-4716-7861-5
33. MARXISM, SOCIALISM & COMMUNISM, ISBN: 978-1-4716-8236-0

Andreas Sofroniou

www.ingramcontent.com/pod-product-compliance
Lightning Source LLC
Chambersburg PA
CBHW052103270326
41931CB00012B/2861

WHY YOU SHOULD GIVE UP

Caffeine

AND HOW TO DO IT

WHY YOU SHOULD GIVE UP

Caffeine

AND HOW TO DO IT

James Downie

Why You Should Give Up Caffeine And How To Do It

See other books by the Author at his Amazon author page:
www.amazon.com/author/bestselling

Published by Blue Peg Publishing

If you have purchased the ebook version of this book, then please consider buying the print version if your family enjoys the ebook.

Contents

CHAPTER ONE

Why You Need To Be Concerned About Caffeine

It's 7 a.m. and the rain has been falling steadily since you left the warmth of your bed. You got about four of the seven to nine hours of sleep you need to function because when the baby wasn't crying your three-year-old whimpered with a bad cold.

You shuffle impatiently. How long does it take to pour a bit of java into a cup anyhow?

The line at the coffee shop is long and slow-moving. But you need that caffeine like a drowning person needs a life jacket. It will make the day seem bearable, send warmth through your veins and give you that little shot of energy that will get you going.

You have a little nagging feeling inside of you that caffeine dependence might not be your most healthy lifestyle choice, but at this dark and dreary moment, you really don't care.

What is it with the guy ordering the bagel and cream cheese? Doesn't he know how long that takes while all these people are waiting?

You remember how American humorist Dave Barry describes a coffee line-up.

"It is inhumane, in my opinion, to force people who have a genuine medical need for coffee to wait in line behind people who apparently view it as some kind of recreational activity," he writes.

"I bet this kind of thing does not happen to heroin addicts. I bet that when serious addicts go to purchase their heroin, they do not tolerate waiting in line while some dilettante in front of them orders a hazelnut smack-a-cino with cinnamon sprinkles."

You are addicted to caffeine and you want it now. It will make everything better.

But how would you feel to find out that it could also make everything worse?

Are you willing to trade that jolt of alertness for the raised blood pressure that accompanies it? Do the good effects on your health weigh favourably against the irritation of your stomach lining and a less effective digestive system?

What if the caffeine filled coffee that makes you wake up is also affecting the length and quality of your sleep? And what if the stimulated blood circulation results in a nervous, jittery feeling that causes your hands to shake and your legs to wobble?

And while your brain is stimulated and you suddenly feel more awake and alive than before, is that too high a price to pay for overworking your pancreas?

In the pages that follow, the impact of caffeine on your body will be outlined. You will see how using too much of this drug can cause cardiovascular problems, stress, blood sugar swings, gastrointestinal problems, and reproductive problems.

You will find out how the amount of caffeine that enters your body through your coffee ritual can unintentionally add up to an overdose.

Most importantly, you will understand the steps you can start right now to reduce your dependency on caffeine and dramatically change your life.

The flicker of a thought that caffeine is not good for you may cross your mind, but it's still Monday, it's still raining, and your kids still kept you awake half the night.

You just know you want your coffee. You need your coffee. It will make you better.

And you have lots of company.

You have all the other people in this line and all the other lines at the other shops and standing in the office cafeterias and coffee counters at corner stores. You have the long distance driver grabbing the energy drink as a soul mate, and also the person who can't even wait for the water to boil and instead just chugs down their cola drink.

Around the world, people drink an estimated 120,000 tonnes of caffeine every year.

In the United States alone, approximately 80 to 90 percent of the teen-age and adult population use caffeine on a daily basis, making it the most widely used drug in their society, exceeding even nicotine and alcohol. Annual consumption per capita is more than four kilograms (8.8 pounds).

Consumption in Europe ranges from about 10 kilograms (22 pounds) in the Nordic countries of Denmark, Finland, Iceland, Norway and Sweden) to around three kilograms (6.6 pounds) in the United Kingdom.

In Australia, there is evidence of a rapidly growing coffee culture. Australians are projected to spend $773.5 million on coffee beans and instant coffee for brewing at home this year and almost $800 million in 2013.

We love our caffeine because it is a natural stimulant that increases our alertness. The effects of caffeine begin about 15 minutes after you consume it, and they last for several hours. You forget your sleep deprivation. The caffeine is stimulating the cortex of your brain, heightening the intensity of your mental activities. You feel warmer as it stimulates your blood circulation.

And even if it is a drug, it's not an illegal drug. So where's the harm?

So you make it through your day, lidded cup in hand, your little security blanket in a tough cold world. You refill it for your meetings, with your lunch, around 2:30 p.m. when you want to nod off for a nap, and you grab one for the road at the work day's end.

And you see lots of others doing the same thing. It is all part of our great caffeine culture and it's almost as old as time.

The famous and influential 19th century playwright and writer Honore de Balzac drank coffee by the continual pot so he could stay up for days, drinking alcohol and writing.

In his essay *The Pleasures and Pains of Coffee*, he detailed the impact his habit had on him.

"The state coffee puts one in when it is drunk on an empty stomach under these magisterial conditions produces a kind of animation that looks like anger: one's voice rises, one's gestures suggest unhealthy impatience: one wants everything to proceed with the speed of ideas: one become brusque, ill-tempered about nothing."

Caffeine dependence impacts people at all educational and financial levels in life. Celebrities like Elton John, Victoria Beckham and former US President Bill Clinton all admit to being hooked on diet soda, joining the ranks of millions of North Americans.

Coffee remains the preferred source of caffeine for the largest segment of the population, however. A new study by Dunkin' Donuts and CareerBuilder found that scientists, public relations people and school administrators were the top three coffee consumers among professions.

Writers and editors came in fourth, and health care administrators, doctors and food preparers ranged fifth, sixth and seventh respectively. The top 10 consumers' list was completed with professor at eight, social workers at nine and financial professionals at 10.

Regardless of their professions, 46 percent of all workers in the United States claimed that they are more productive with coffee. And 61 percent of the workers who need coffee to get through their days drink more than two cups.

Should you be worried about the caffeine that you consume? Based on a number of scientific studies, the answer is yes. Anything more than a moderate intake of caffeine can lead to long-term health issues from cardiovascular attacks to increased stress to blood sugar swings.

Caffeine can lead to gastrointestinal difficulties, nutritional deficiencies, and adrenal exhaustion.

Every time you ingest this powerful drug, you are overriding your body's natural systems and directly impacting your physical performance and psychological health. This physical stimulant can intoxicate you in massive doses, and in extreme cases, cause death.

Caffeine consumption, intensified with the growing popularity of coffee shops and energy drinks, may be part of our culture, but it is not a healthy part of it.

In the coming chapters, you will learn what caffeine does to your body and your mind. You will find out what happens when you keep your body is a state of perpetual stimulation.

The impacts of caffeine are as individual as you are, but we can offer some clues and measurements to help determine the specific ways in which caffeine affects you personally.

We will look at the latest scientific studies into caffeine consumption and its consequences. We will give you the tools to determine how much caffeine you are ingesting each day and find out if you are in danger of becoming drunk on caffeine.

Finally, if you make the decision that you want to reduce or eliminate caffeine from your life, this book will help you set up your own personal strategy for quitting.

CHAPTER TWO

How Caffeine Became The World's Most Popular Drug

Coffee remains our favourite source of caffeine, and a good strong cuppa' is the foundation of many of our life and work routines.

And while consumption has steadily increased each year, it has always been popular. Even writer T. S. Eliot once mused that he had "measured out my life with coffee spoons."

German chemist Friedlieb Ferdinand Runge is credited as being the first scientist to isolate caffeine from coffee, followed a year later by French chemists Pierre Robiquet, Pierre Pelletier and Joseph Caventou.

It was Pelletier who coined the word "cafeine" from the French word for coffee (cafe) and this word evolved into the English version, "caffeine."

According to the International Coffee Association's historical archives, the global spread of coffee growing and drinking began in the Horn of Africa, specifically in the Ethiopian province of Kaffa where coffee trees originated. The fruit of the plant, known as a coffee cherry, was eaten by slaves taken from present day Sudan into Yemen and Arabia through what was then a great port, Mocha.

There are accounts of coffee being cultivated in Yemen by the 15th century, but historians speculate it was likely being grown much earlier. The Arabs originally banned the export of coffee beans, but by 1616 the ban had been circumvented and the Dutch were growing coffee in greenhouses in the Netherlands.

The very first of the "coffee houses" as we know them began in Yemen and they were immediately popular. While drinking coffee, people played chess, exchanged gossip, sang songs and enjoyed music. Over time, they also became a centre for political activity and were subsequently banned, but they kept reappearing until a cultural acceptance was found.

Coffee's popularity around the world continued to grow, thanks in large part to the Dutch. By the late 1600s, they were growing coffee at Malabar in India and by 1699 took some plants to Batavia in Java, in what is now Indonesia. In a relatively short period of time, the Dutch colonies were the main suppliers of coffee to Europe. Around this time, two other popular caffeine-containing beverages were introduced: hot chocolate and tea.

The "coffee culture" started to put down roots and grow more rapidly than it seemed possible. The first European coffeehouse opened in Venice in 1683, with the most famous, Caffee Florian in Piazza San Marco opening in 1720. Unbelievably it is still open today at 56 30124 Venice, Italy (041-520-5641).

The largest insurance market in the world, Lloyd's of London, began life as a coffeehouse in 1688, started by Edward Lloyd, who prepared lists of the ships that his customers had insured.

By 1668, there were literary references to coffee being consumed in North America and shortly after that coffee houses grew popular in New York, Philadelphia, Boston and other towns.

Ironically, the famous Boston Tea Party of 1773 was planned in the Green Dragon, a coffee house. Both the New York Stock Exchange and the Bank of New York started in coffeehouses where Wall Street is today.

Meanwhile, the Dutch spread the coffee plant to Central and South America, and today it remains their main cash crop.

For American coffee drinkers, it was their wettest city, Seattle that became synonymous with a new type of cafe culture in the 1970s. As Amazon.com founder Jeff Bezos quipped: "In Seattle you haven't had enough coffee until you can thread a sewing machine while it's running."

In the years that followed, massive chains of coffee shops with standardized quality and cup sizes spread like only a caffeine-high business could.

Before long, by volume alone, the United States was the largest market in the world for coffee, with a Starbucks or one of its other franchised competitors on every corner. Germany and Japan followed in consumption.

Canada, Australia and New Zealand quickly took their places as large coffee consuming countries. In Canada, the Tim Horton's coffee chain has become emblematic of the entire Canadian culture and it makes millions of cups of coffee each day.

While the Nordic countries continue to consume the most coffee per capita, even the traditionally tea-drinking United Kingdom is seeing rapid growth in coffee consumption.

The more coffee shops are built, the more people line up to get into them. Coffee is the new social lubricant of our society. Coffee shops are the taverns for non-drinkers.

We are a stimulated society as a result. We go to the coffee shop to take away our cup of comfort or drink it there with friends. Sometimes we just want to have a jolt of energy while we surf the Internet or read. Either way, the coffee shop is our home away from home.

The influence of caffeine consumption is felt strongly in our work places as well. Many contracts for workers actually stipulate for mandatory "coffee breaks." While the term actually dates back to the 19th century in Stoughton, Wisconsin when female

Norwegian immigrants took time out for coffee, it shot into popular culture in 1951 when *Time* magazine reported that since the war, "the coffee break has been written into union contracts."

In 1952, the popularity of the practice and the phrase was cemented through a Pan-American Coffee Bureau ad campaign which urged consumers to "Give Yourself A Coffee-Break --- And Get What Coffee Gives To You."

Our caffeine-braced culture continues to entrench itself in magazine articles, in books, and in popular television shows. *NCIS* show characters can't start their day without coffee in their hands, and the handsome murder mystery writer Richard Castle of the crime drama *Castle* endears himself to co-worker Kate Beckett each morning with a steaming hot cup of coffee. The long-running series *Friends* was full of coffee-drinking and coffee references, as was *Frasier*.

Popular comic strips like "Adam" and "Pearls Before Swine" revolve around the goings-on of visits and work at coffee shops.

Today figures for global consumption of caffeine translate to one caffeinated beverage for every person on this planet every day.

Although coffee is a principle source of caffeine, other popular sources are tea, cola drinks, chocolate derived from cocoa beans, energy drinks and even inhaled caffeine and caffeine tablets. Many common medications also contain caffeine.

There is no denying that caffeine has engrained itself deeply into the social fabric of our culture. But what is it doing to us as a result?

CHAPTER THREE

What Caffeine Does To Your Body

If you drink a moderate amount of coffee or cola daily (two to three cups), there is no unchallenged scientific evidence that conclusively shows you are endangering your health. In fact, a few studies have shown small health benefits from your coffee habit.

While this is reassuring if you are not motivated now to walk away from your caffeine crutch at this time, it should not be construed as an endorsement of caffeine.

The reality is that study after study suggests over a prolonged period of time that caffeine consumption will cause you harm, spiking your blood pressure, over-working your pancreas, slowing your liver and aging your kidneys.

Caffeine is also an addictive drug, and the more you take it and enjoy its effects, the more you want and need to heighten the feeling of energy and well-being that follows its consumption.

Within an hour after drinking a caffeinated beverage, the drug is in your tissues and your blood stream and it stays there for between five and six hours. During that time, as it works its way through your body, it causes changes to occur.

Caffeine acts on a number of parts of our body, but its chief impact is that it counteracts a substance called adenosine. This naturally circulates at high levels throughout the body and in the nervous system.

What adenosine does is act as an inhibitor neurotransmitter that diminishes and suppresses activity in the central nervous system. When you drink coffee or a cola, you upset the adenosine, making it increase its activity.

Upsetting the adenosine is significant because it is involved in a wide range of essential bodily functions. It regulates the cardiovascular system, the renal system, the respiratory systems, and the central neuro-system. Caffeine competes with the adenosine for control of these vital systems.

When caffeine occupies adenosine sites in the body, it pushes for an increase in functionality. But adenosine, functioning without competition from caffeine, actually does the opposite; it works to slow things down. That conflict between the caffeine and adenosine is where that feeling of stimulation comes from after drinking coffee or cola.

Caffeine increases your heart rate, elevates your blood pressure and increases your cholesterol and homocysteine, a biochemical linked to increased risk of heart attack.

Feeling jittery after your "large double double?" That is because caffeine stimulates your stress hormones and that in turn leads to increased levels of anxiety, irritability, muscle tension and pain, indigestion, insomnia and decreased immunity.

Caffeine also creates swings in your blood sugar. It stimulates a temporary surge in blood sugar which is then followed by an overproduction of insulin and that causes a blood sugar crash within hours.

This is particularly vital if you are diabetic of hypoglycemic, but it is also of concern to people trying to lose weight. Even though you have decreased your caloric intake and increased your exercise regime, your weight loss may stall if you continue to ingest large amounts of coffee or diet cola since your insulin is simultaneously sending a message to your body to store your extra sugar as fat. When your blood sugar gets low, you will find yourself craving food, especially sweets.

And that is not all caffeine does to your body.

Ever had a burning sensation in the pit of your stomach after you pulled an all-nighter fuelled by coffee? That's because the caffeine filled coffee hikes the secretion of hydrochloric acid. The result is making you vulnerable to ulcers. Large amounts of coffee also contribute to another gastrointestinal problem called gastro-esophageal reflux disease.

Caffeine also slows or stops the absorption of essential nutrients by your body, and excretes calcium, magnesium, potassium, iron and trace minerals through your urine.

The constant over-stimulation of your body for a prolonged period also makes you at risk for eventual adrenal exhaustion, making you susceptible to inflammation, autoimmunity, depression and mood imbalances.

Caffeine hikes the level of the stress hormone cortisol in the blood for up to 18 hours, and it is a stress hormone.

Some studies have also shown that caffeine dehydrates the body and makes our skin age more rapidly. It also ages our kidneys and inhibits DNA repair, and even affects our liver. It makes our livers slower to detoxify foreign toxins.

People have different sensitivity levels to caffeine as well, so what is moderate for one may be over the top for another.

According to health experts at the Mayo Clinic, even if you don't drink coffee regularly, even a cup of it will spike your blood pressure. That is because caffeine prevents your arteries from widening and increases your adrenaline levels, all which slightly elevate your blood pressure.

Their recommendation is that your caffeinated coffee consumption not exceed more than 24 ounces a day.

Caffeine can also prevent you from falling into a healthy sleep at night. When you do sleep, it shortens the amount of time you stay in slumber and increases the number of times you wake up during the night. All of this interferes with a normal restorative sleep pattern.

Are you still willing to risk all of this for that extra jolt of energy it gives you to make it through the day?

Scientists are now suggesting that even that feeling may all be an illusion.

A United Kingdom study published in 2010 in the medical journal *Neuropsychopharmacology* suggested that the notion that caffeine makes us more alert is more imagined than real and that frequent coffee drinkers develop a tolerance to both its stimulatory and anxiety-producing effects.

Researchers at Bristol University concluded that while frequent coffee drinkers may feel alerted by coffee, this is just a sign of reversing the fatigue effect of caffeine withdrawal, and given that caffeine also increases anxiety and blood pressure, there is no net advantage.

"Our study shows that we don't gain an advantage from consuming caffeine - although we feel alerted by it, this is caffeine just bringing us back to normal," lead research Dr. Peter Rogers of the Department of Experimental Psychology said at the time.

"On the other hand, while caffeine can increase anxiety, tolerance means that for most caffeine consumers this effect is negligible," he added.

They concluded that:

"With frequent consumption, substantial tolerance develops to the anxiogenic effect of caffeine, even in genetically susceptible individuals, but no net benefit for alertness is gained, as caffeine abstinence reduces alertness and consumption merely returns it to baseline."

The International Food information Council Foundation, in a landmark report called "Caffeine And Health: Clarifying The Controversies," ultimately concluded that moderate intake of

300 mg a day (about three cups of coffee) did not cause adverse health effects in healthy adults.

However, their researchers found that some groups, particularly those with hypertension and the elderly, may be more vulnerable.

The message of caution has also been repeated by such leading institutions as Johns Hopkins and the Mayo Clinic. Both have urged people with existing heart problems to stay away from caffeine.

In their warning, they also signal out people who already have an elevated blood pressure, those who are already on hypertension medication and those suffering from cardiovascular disease.

How Much Stimulating Is Safe For You?

Eighteen year old Zoe Cross loved the stimulating buzz she got from drinking a popular cola so she gradually kept increasing her consumption until she was gulping down 18 pints (288 ounces) of it a day for four years straight.

Her quest for constant stimulation ended up with her in the hospital, suffering from an E. Coli infection which was possibly linked to drinking straight from unwashed cans and exacerbated by her extreme dehydration.

According to a story in *The Sun* newspaper, Zoe ended up on a saline drip for five days. The doctors told her that her body couldn't cope with such a huge amount of caffeine and sugar, and they warned her that her kidneys could shut down if she didn't quit her habit.

News reports in recent years have also centred on the growing popularity of caffeine laced energy drinks such as Red Bull or Monster, and even inhaled caffeine dispensers. These drinks come in containers smaller than the average soda can, according to Johns Hopkins researchers, but they contain two to four times as much caffeine.

Studies conducted by the American Heart Association showed that volunteers who regularly consumed energy drinks experienced their heart rates spiking five to seven beats a minute.

What happened to the average long-time consumer of caffeinated drinks? How does the push for prolonged stimulation impact on the body?

In the previous chapter, we talked about how caffeine competes with adenosine and tries to speed up our body systems as opposed to slowing them down.

When you drink coffee regularly, the number of adenosine receptors in your body increase to balance out the ones being occupied by caffeine. What happens next is that if you miss your coffee for a day or try to quit permanently, you end up with an oversupply of adenosine receptors and this makes quitting a most unpleasant process.

It means you will have excessive tiredness, lethargy, irritability and headaches.

The cycle of caffeine dependency and its negative impacts on your body plays out day in and day out, however, even if you are a regular coffee drinker and aren't trying to quit. The time it takes caffeine to move through your system is about five hours. Most people reach for another cup through the day at regular intervals, but they begin to taper off their use in the late afternoon or early evening.

That leaves a period of about 12 to 14 hours without their bodies getting a fresh dose of caffeine, so by the time they wake up in the morning, their bodies are crying out for that first cup of coffee or tea or cola to help them wake up. Many caffeine users wake up with a mild to severe headache.

If you are a normal coffee drinker, chances are you are not over-stimulating your body, because there is a level of consumption that suddenly becomes unpleasant. Most people will drive between two and five cups a day, for example, but a few will drink 10 to 12 and a small few who go up as high as 20 to 30 cups.

If the person who normally drinks five cups suddenly drinks 20 cups, their will generally feel so uncomfortable that they will immediately reduce their consumption the next day.

In that way, our bodies tend to maintain their own check on how much stimulation we allow ourselves.

There is another gauge for how much coffee you will feel comfortable drinking, and that is how quickly it moves through your system and leaves as urine. As a general rule, people who eliminate their caffeine quite quickly can consume more than those who eliminate it slower.

So what is "right" and what is "wrong" when it comes to sensible coffee consumption and determining how much stimulation feels great and how much crosses the line to discomfort?

Here is the conundrum:

Unlike other drugs that depend on amount for impact on your body, caffeine affects you the same whether you drink one cup or 10. Each cup elicits the same hike in blood pressure, whether it is your first of the day or your tenth.

The bottom line is thus not how much you can safely consume for the stimulation level that you seek, but whether you should consume it at all. If you do not want your body to be impacted by hikes in blood pressure and the other changes that accompany caffeine, then you need to stop consumption completely, not just decrease it.

Making such a decision is a lifestyle choice, not just a food or beverage choice. Most of us don't take it lightly.

What we can do is read on and learn more about what caffeine does to our minds and impacts us as individuals to help us make our choice.

CHAPTER FIVE

What Caffeine Is Doing To Your Mind

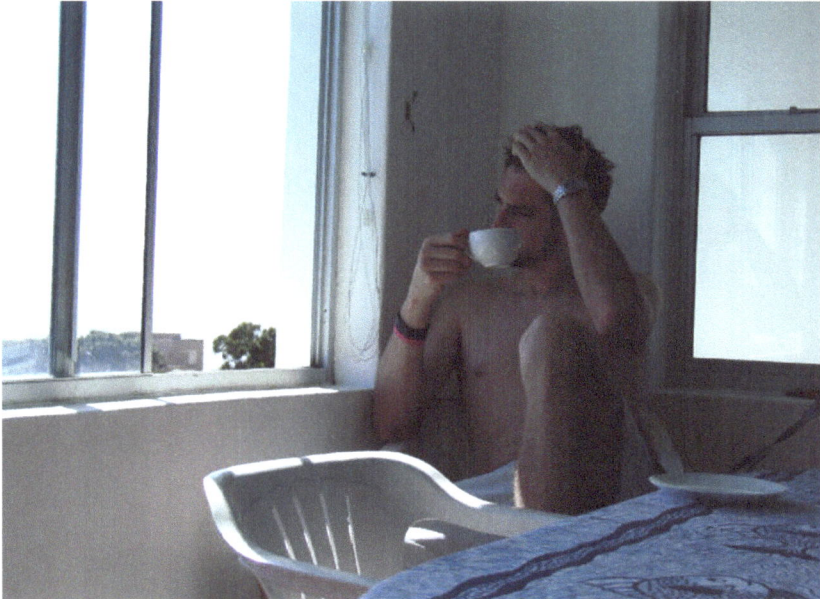

Contrary to popular belief, caffeine isn't the "gas" that fuels your brain, sharpening its responses and quickening its calculating time. Instead, it is actually a dead weight holding down the brain's normal responses, keeping them from doing their job properly and giving you a false sense of alertness.

One of the best explanations of what caffeine is doing to your mind is by Stephen R. Braun in a 224-page treatise called *The Science and Lore of Alcohol and Caffeine* released in 1997 but just as relevant today as it ever was.

The essence of his scientific argument is that the relationship between the human brain and the impact of caffeine is universally misunderstood. It is not how caffeine works on our brain that gives us a sense of alertness; rather, it is how caffeine prevents our brain from functioning as it was intended that results in the changes we perceive.

From the moment you wake up in the morning, the neurons in your brain get fired up and start producing adenosine, a valuable by-product that controls the functioning of your entire nervous system. If the adenosine gets low, it sends a signal to tell your body it would be product to slow down and take it easy for a few minutes. When its supply is stabilized, you have lots of normal energy and strength to complete your task at hand.

It is really a marvellously efficient and well-operated system that prepares you for a long and active life. But for most of us, we believe we can improve a bit on what nature intended, and so we reach for our cup of caffeine.

And then our system starts to break down.

That is because caffeine is the superb impersonator of adenosine. It mimic's adenosine's size and shape and enters the receptors. It binds to it, but doesn't activate it; instead, it acts as a kind of brake on the system, at least temporarily. So your brain tells you that even though you haven't had sufficient sleep for five nights and you are running on empty, it's okay; you can just keep on chugging for a few more hours. It doesn't change the bad impact such a lifestyle is having on your body and your entire nervous system; it just pushes it to function a little further.

The result in your brain is complicated. Caffeine isn't as direct an influence as an amphetamine or cocaine that operates as a stimulant.

Instead, while it pushes you to keep going, it doesn't push you to be more skilled or better at what you are doing. It just allows you to do more of the same. If your job is totally routine, caffeine can allow you to keep at it and fight fatigue for long hours. It has been shown to even help you remember things and retain what you are learning.

Braun speculates that part of that memory retention may be spurred by the body's increased production of adrenalin when you drink caffeine. When all of us find ourselves in fight or flight situations and our adrenalin is peaking, we remember the horror of it all for the rest of our lives. To prove this, just ask people if they can remember where they were when U.S. President John F. Kennedy was shot, or when John Lennon was assassinated, or where they were when the Twin Towers were attached in New York City?

But does caffeine boost your creativity or complicated skill output? Are those agents on *NCIS* more likely to zero in on the key to the crime they are solving because they are constantly guzzling coffee? Not likely. Caffeine can make you work faster and longer, but not better.

Not only that, its impact is not consistent. It varies from person to person, altered by genetics and other factors such as the medication you are taking and whether or not you are also a smoker.

There is also the sobering reality that even though caffeine can ward off that feeling of sleepiness for many hours, the effect won't last forever. Eventually, your nervous system just crashes in exhaustion. It is still the ultimate controller and it pays to remember that.

Signals that your nervous system is over-extended as you continue to ingest caffeine are trembling, anxiety and general nervousness. It may become impossible to relax and even more impossible to sleep deeply.

To complicate your assessment of what caffeine is doing to your brain still further, consider that its impact keeps changing the longer you maintain a caffeine habit.

For example repeated studies show that as we become tolerant to our daily doses of caffeine, it becomes a little less effective, and we have a tendency to add an extra shot to return ourselves to that "buzzed" feeling.

Tolerance can set in as early as a week to 12 days of establishing a coffee habit. Ironically, if we add more caffeine to increase a feeling of energy, it doesn't work. Whether we are drinking three cups or six cups, our brain is reacting pretty much the same way.

The only change will be how bad you feel when you suddenly decide to stop or are forced to by other circumstances.

A bad headache is the universal signal of caffeine withdrawal, and it hits with full fury within 12 to 24 hours after your last cup of coffee. Your brain is reacting with shock and disbelief, because all of a sudden, it is being asked to function in a completely different way again.

You are likely to experience depression, fatigue, lethargy, irritability, nausea, and vomiting and even eye muscle spasms as your brain struggles to revert to its former system of handling your nervous system.

If you have specific medical conditions or are certain medications, the impact can be even more pronounced as we will discuss in the next chapter.

How Caffeine Impacts You As An Individual

As you are now aware, caffeine impacts on you as an individual in a specific way, different from your co-workers, your friends and even others in your family.

For the average user, the results are alluring. This central nervous system and metabolic stimulant appears to produce increased wakefulness, more focused and clear thoughts, and overall better body coordination.

But even for the generally healthy users, it affects them in different ways. Many coffee drinkers suffer from some form of insomnia.

High doses of caffeine have been found to impair athletic performance by interfering with coordination.

But what if you ingest caffeine when you are already in a physically compromised state?

If you are a diabetic, a heart patient, an asthmatic or taking birth control pills, does it make a difference to what caffeine does to your body?

The general answer is yes, and in this chapter we will look at some of the specific common conditions that cause caffeine to react in either a positive or negative fashion.

For example, if you are already taking medications for pain, obesity, hypertension or depression, you should not drink coffee at all, since it may well eliminate any good the medicine is doing you.

If you have a high fever from a flu or infection, you should definitely avoid drinking caffeine. Reach for the lemon juice instead.

If you are taking medication for high blood pressure, be aware that within two hours of ingesting caffeine in any form, your blood pressure rises and stays high for nearly three hours. If you have a coffee habit that requires a cup about every three or four hours during your day, then you are constantly over-riding the medication, and are keeping your blood pressure high all day. Among the health effects of this will be a general feeling of edginess and anxiety.

Woman taking birth control pills need about twice as much time as others to process caffeine in their bodies. Women between the ovulation and beginning of menstruation also see a similar lengthening of time caffeine is kept in their bodies.

Conversely, people who smoke regularly process caffeine much quicker than other users, which may be behind the statistic that smokers drink more coffee than non-smokers. Smokers are also more apt to feel more agitated and anxious.

Health Canada, after a massive review of scientific literature about the impact of caffeine on our bodies, concluded that children are at increased risk for possible behavioural effects from caffeine and that women of childbearing age are at increased risk of possible reproductive effects.

There is no hard and fast evidence to conclude that caffeine consumption during pregnancy increases the risk of congenital malformations or growth retardation when it is consumed in moderate amounts.

To stay within their recommended limit, a pregnant woman could drink a little more than two eight-ounce cups of coffee a day, as long as she did not take any other products that have caffeine in them.

However, keep in mind that just one take-out coffee of 20 ounces would contain more caffeine than the daily limit suggested for pregnant women.

The United Kingdom Food Standards Agency recommends that pregnant women should not drink more than 200 mg of caffeine a day, the equivalent of one and a half cups of fresh coffee.

The scientists urging cautious consumption or none at all during pregnancy are concerned about a growing pool of evidence that the hormonal changes linked to pregnancy slow the metabolic clearance of caffeine from the woman's system, making a normal dose of caffeine last much longer.

For people suffering from anxiety disorders, science also bring mixed messages about caffeine use. In clinical studies, some people with panic disorder had a positive response to caffeine, while others who were ordered to quit caffeine showed considerable less anxiety in the long run.

All studies showed that at doses higher than 300 mg a day, caffeine worsened patient anxiety and even trigger mania and psychosis.

People who over-indulge in coffee can also develop a deficiency in thiamine or Vitamin B1, and this causes fatigue and nervousness, as well as aches and pains and headaches.

Excessive coffee drinking can also bring about an increased risk of osteoporosis. It uses up the calcium in the body and simultaneous causes increased excretion of calcium in our urine. The final result is that coffee drinkers deplete their calcium reserves and face increased risk of osteoporosis. This is not only a particular problem for post-menopausal women but also for men.

For heart patients, a warning about caffeine use is standard. According to Harvard University Medical School, excessive caffeine consumption can prompt arrhythmia, otherwise known as irregular heart beat.

A jolt of caffeine can also increase your heart rate.

Furthermore, caffeine's tendency to contribute to hypertension, or high blood pressure, put the heart patient in particular at risk for heart disease and strokes.

If you have liver problems, caffeine is also something to be avoided. It combines with hydrochloric acid in your stomach to create a toxin called caffeine hydrochloride. It is absorbed by your liver, which must then neutralize it and eliminate it from your system. Sometimes as the liver processes these toxins it can incur tissue damage and form scar tissue, and this will ultimately hinder your liver from functioning as it should.

If you have asthma and use caffeine heavily prior to having your lung function tested, there is the possibility that it will give a false reading.

That is because caffeine is very similar to a drug called theophylline, a bronchodilator that relieves symptoms of asthma like wheezing, coughing and breathlessness.

What scientists are studying now is to determine whether caffeine has the same effect on lungs as theophylline. This is significant knowledge, because if it does, people with asthma may actually be encouraged to consume caffeine.

In the meantime, there is a serious concern that heavy caffeine users who also have asthma may be masking how bad their asthma is when they have tests taken. If caffeine acts as a bronchodilator and widens the airways, then the patient may appear in a test to be breathing more easily than the doctor anticipated.

That can lead to the doctor prescribing a smaller dose or weaker drug than the patient really needs, which will lead long term to serious issues with asthma management or in the extreme, a fatal attack.

Nor is it reasonable for the person with asthma to conclude that caffeine is an acceptable replacement for their other medications. To have the same impact, it may be necessary for them to absorb such massive amounts of caffeine that it harms other bodily systems.

CHAPTER SEVEN

Can You Get Drunk On Caffeine?

At an emergency room in Berkeley, California in 2005, Dr. Guy Shochat treated an 18-year-old who had arrived in an ambulance with sudden heart arrhythmia.

According to a story in *The New York Times*, the teenager had been drinking eight 16-ounce cans of the caffeinated energy drink Rockstar every evening to stay awake for his night job.

It was one of the first widely-publicized cases of caffeine poisoning in North America and the beginning of a growing trend.

By 2008 in the United States alone there were 5,448 cases of caffeine poisoning on the record, and one death resulted from it, according to the American Association of Poison Control Centers.

It was becoming shockingly clear that an overdose of caffeine, like any other drug, could be fatal. It was also evident that people could become intoxicated on caffeine and unable to function normally.

According to the American Psychiatric Association, symptoms that you have over-dosed on caffeine include the following:

- You are restless.
- You are nervous.
- You are excited.
- You have insomnia.
- You have a flushed face.
- You have nausea or vomiting.
- Your muscles are twitching.
- You have increased urination.
- You have a rambling flow of thought and speech.
- You have rapid or irregular heartbeat.
- You have periods of inexhaustibility.
- You have convulsions and confusion.

Symptoms in babies and small children include nausea, rapid, deep breathing, rapid heartbeat, shock, tremors and vomiting. Their muscles may be very tense, and then very relaxed.

Acute caffeine poisoning gives early symptoms of anorexia, tremor and restlessness. It is followed by nausea, vomiting, irregular heartbeats and confusion. Serious intoxication from caffeine leaves you in a state of delirium with seizures and palpitations.

Being drunk on caffeine is commonly referred to as the "caffeine jitters."

How much caffeine does it take for you to enter this dangerous state of super-buzz?

A median lethal dose in people is hard to measure since caffeine impacts us individually. However, it is estimated to be about 150 to 200 milligrams per kilogram of body mass.

In practical terms, that means the equivalent of between 80 to 100 cups of coffee for an average adult. While that may sound impossible to achieve, victims of caffeine poisoning reach that dose unintentionally by combining coffee or cola with caffeine pills to stay awake during times of intense stress.

A death from caffeine overdose would normally be caused by ventricular fibrillation, meaning the caffeine caused the cardiovascular system to overwork to a point that it could no longer function.

Much less caffeine would be required to be a toxic amount for a small child (about 35 mg could be fatal). An average cup of coffee contains about 50 to 200 mg. The difference in toxic levels in children and adults comes from the fact that infants and very young children metabolize caffeine very slowly.

Emergency treatment of a person with caffeine poisoning involves maintaining the airway and assisting in ventilation, treating seizures and monitoring vital signs. Medical personnel administer beta blockers to reverse the effects of the over-stimulation.

Often vomiting is induced or a gastric lavage performed. The latter is when a tube is inserted through the nose into the stomach to wash out the stomach. The patient will also receive activated charcoal.

If you are at home waiting for medical care, do not make the caffeine intoxicated person throw up unless a poison control official or a doctor has instructed you to do so.

If you are about to call for emergency assistance, be ready to describe the intoxicated person's age, weight and condition, the name of the product they have been ingesting and the amounts if you can determine that, the time period they ingested the caffeine and the amount from different sources (coffee and caffeine pills combined, for example.)

Remember the average adult can usually drink between two to four cups of brewed coffee every day without becoming caffeine drunk. But the mixture of other medications and circumstances and body types can mean that you are at risk.

If you are drinking four or more cups of coffee a day and you are experiencing sleeplessness, nervousness, restlessness, irritability, stomach upset, a fast heartbeat and muscle tremors, you are entering the danger zone.

Sleeplessness is defined by getting less than seven to eight hours of sleep each night. If you chronically cannot sleep sufficient hours, you will end up with sleep deprivation and this will disturb your daytime performance and alertness. Sleep loss is cumulative, so remember that if you are constantly upping your caffeine content to get through a crisis or finish a big project, for example, you can be doing long-term damage to your health.

When you overdose on caffeine to make up for loss of sleep, you will find that a vicious cycle starts to develop. Because sleep loss is cumulative, after a while you need even more caffeine to stay alert during the day. While you reach for even more coffee, cola or energy drinks or even caffeine pills, they ultimately take control of your body, making it impossible for you to sleep long periods at night. The length of time for your sleep correspondingly gets shorter and short until the chronic sleeplessness undermines your overall health and alertness.

You can accidentally become drunk on caffeine by mixing them with other medications if you are unaware of what happens in your body with certain drugs.

For example, if you take two common antibiotics, ciprofloxacin (Cipro) and norfloxacin (Noroxin), caffeine in your body will remain there much longer than normal, and its unwanted effects will be dramatically increased.

If you have breathing difficulties and are prescribed bronchodilators such as theophylline (Theo-24) or elixophyllin, among others, drinking caffeine-laced beverages may give you heart palpitations and nausea or vomiting.

Many people take an herbal supplement called Echinacea because it is believed to help them prevent colds and other infections. Unknown to them, this herb also increases the concentration of caffeine in their blood and heightens its effects on them.

How Much Caffeine Are You Taking In Each Day?

Caffeine has captured the world as the drug of choice for millions of people. It crosses all geographic and cultural boundaries. It defies diplomatic ties and economic realities.

It is our universal cup of comfort.

It is written about and talked about and offered as an accepted gesture of welcome. It is a reason for people to meet, to share their days and their dreams and ambitions.

It is an elemental part of our social fabric.

A Turkish proverb eloquently describes coffee as something that should be "black as hell, strong as death, and sweet as love."

A coffee shop in United States posted an anonymous version of coffee adoration modelled after the 23rd Psalm.

The first four lines were:

> "Caffeine is my shepherd; I shall not doze.
> It maketh me to wake in green pastures:
> It leadeth me beyond the sleeping masses.
> It restoreth my buzz."

Caffeine is so engrained in our lives that it is hard to imagine our days without it.

But when taken in excess, it can also damage our overall health and destroy us. It can move us from our comfort zone to a crisis zone. It can go from a joyous jolt of energy into a dangerous spiral of sickness and even death.

We have learned that many caffeine poisonings are accidental. That leads to the question: how much caffeine are we really ingesting each day?

According to Mayo Clinic staff, if you are ingesting more than 500 milligrams of caffeine each day, you need to consider cutting back.

How much is that in product terms?

A cup of regular coffee has about 100 mg of caffeine while a cup of tea has about 50 mg of caffeine. Moderate consumption is considered to be the equivalent of two to three (200-300 mg) cups of coffee per day.

The problems occur when we mix the caffeine that we are conscious of consuming with the hidden caffeine in other drinks, foods and medications that we are unaware of.

For example, caffeine is also found in iced tea, cocoa, chocolate and soft drinks as well as in over the counter drugs.

Two tables of Anacin has 64 mg of caffeine, 2 tablets of Excedrin has 130 mg.

One table of NoDoz: Regular Strength, has 100 mg of caffeine, and one table of Maximum Strength has 200 mg. One tablet of caffedrine has 200 mg, as does one table of Vivarin.

One tablet of Midol has 64 mg, while one table of Dexatrim has 200 mg.

A Red Bull has 80 mg of caffeine, while a 12 ounce can of Diet Coke has 47 mg. A 12 ounce Mountain Dew has 54 mg while a 12 ounce Dr. Pepper has 42 mg.

A cup of hot chocolate has 14 mg, while a 12 ounce iced tea has 70 mg.

An Expresso has 100 mg of caffeine while an eight ounce chocolate bar has about 8 mg.

More than 20 per cent of adult men and 15 per cent of adult women in Canada exceed the recommended maximum daily intake of 400 mg of caffeine per day. And that country is not unique, and in fact, is not even one of the top coffee-drinking nations.

The Centre for Science in the Public Interest has gathered detailed information about caffeine content in common foods, beverages and medications.

Here are some common foods and beverages that have caffeine that you might be failing to consider in calculating your daily intake:

Coffees

Coffee, generic brewed – 8 ounces – 133 mg
Coffee, generic instant – 8 ounces – 93 mg
Starbucks Brewed Coffee (Grande) – 16 ounces – 320 mg
Einstein Bros. regular coffee – 16 ounces – 300 mg
Dunkin' Donuts regular coffee – 16 ounces – 206 mg
Starbucks Vanilla Latte (Grande) – 16 ounces – 150 mg
Starbucks Espresso, dopplo – 2 ounces – 150 mg
Starbucks Frappuccino Blended Coffee Beverages,
    average – 9.5 ounces – 115 mg
Starbucks Espresso, solo – 1 ounce – 75 mg
Einstein Bros. Espresso – 1 ounce – 75 mg
Espresso, generic – 1 ounce – 40 (range 30-90 mg)
Starbucks Espresso decaffeinated – 1 ounce – 4 mg

Teas

Tea, brewed – 8 ounces – 53 mg (range 40-120 mg)
Starbucks Tazo Chai Tea Latte (Grande) – 16 ounces – 100 mg
Snapple, Lemon (and diet version) – 16 ounces – 42 mg
Snapple, Peace (and diet version) – 16 ounces – 42 mg
Snapple Raspberry (and diet version) – 16 ounces – 42 mg
Arizona Iced Tea, black – 16 ounces – 32 mg

Nestea – 12 ounces – 26 mg

Snapple, Just Plain Unsweetened – 16 ounces – 18 mg

Arizona Iced Tea, green – 16 ounces – 15 mg

Snapple, Kiwi Teawi – 16 ounces – 10 mg

Soft Drinks

FDA official limit for cola and pepper soft drinks – 12 ounces – 71 mg (200 parts per million)

Vault – 12 ounces – 71 mg

Jolt Cola – 12 ounces – 72 mg

Mountain Dew MDX, regular or diet – 12 ounces – 71 mg

Coke Red, regular or diet – 12 ounces – 54 mg

Mountain Dew, regular or diet – 12 ounces – 54 mg

Pepsi One – 12 ounces – 54 mg

Mellow Yellow – 12 ounces – 53 mg

Diet Coke – 12 ounces – 47 mg

TAB – 12 ounces – 47 mg

Pibb Xtra, Diet Mr. Pibb, Pibb Zero – 12 ounces – 41 mg

Dr. Pepper – 12 ounces -42 mg

Dr. Pepper diet – 12 ounces – 44 mg

Pepsi – 12 ounces – 38 mg

Diet Pepsi – 12 ounces – 36 mg

Coca Cola Classic – 12 ounces – 35 mg

Coke Zero – 12 ounces – 35 mg

Barq's Diet Root Beer – 12 ounces – 0 mg

Barq's Root Beer – 12 ounces – 22 mg

7-Up regular or diet – 12 ounces – 0 mg

Fanta, all flavours – 12 ounces – 0 mg

Fresca, all flavours – 12 ounces- 0 mg

Sprite, regular or diet – 12 ounces – 0 mg

Energy Drinks

Spike Shooter – 8.4 ounces – 300 mg
Cocaine – 8.4 ounces – 288 mg
5-Hour Energy – 1.93 ounces – 207 mg
Monster Energy – 16 ounces – 160 mg
Full Throttle – 16 ounces – 144 mg
Rip It, all varieties – 8 ounces – 100 mg
Enviga – 12 ounces – 100 mg
Tab Energy – 10.5 ounces – 95 mg
SoBe No Fear – 8 ounces – 83 mg
Red Bull – 8.3 ounces – 80 mg
Red Bull Sugarfree – 8.3 ounces – 80 mg
Rockstar Energy Drink = 8.3 ounces – 80 mg
SoBe Adrenaline Rush – 8.3 ounces – 79 mg
Amp – 16 ounces – 143 mg
Glaceau Vitamin Water Energy Citrus – 20 ounces – 50 mg
SoBe Essential Energy, Berry or Orange – 8 ounces – 48 mg

Frozen Desserts

Ben & Jerry's Coffee Health Bar Crunch – 8 fluid ounces – 84 mg
Ben & Jerry's Coffee Flavoured Ice Cream – 8 fluid ounces – 68 mg
Haagen-Dazs Coffee Ice Cream – 8 fluid ounces – 58 mg
Haagen-Dazs Coffee Light Ice Cream – 8 fluid ounces – 58 mg
Haagen-Dazs Coffee Frozen Yogurt – 8 fluid ounces – 58 mg
Starbucks Coffee Ice Cream – 8 fluid ounces – 50-60 mg

Chocolates and Candies and Other Drinks

Jolt Caffeinated Gum - 1 stick – 33 mg
Hershey's Special Dark Chocolate Bar – 1.45 ounces – 31 mg
Hershey's Chocolate Bar – 1.55 ounces – 9 mg

Hershey's Kisses – 41 grams (nine pieces) – 9 mg

Hot Cocoa – 8 ounces – 9 mg (range from 3-13 mg)

Chocolate milk – 8 ounces – 8 mg

Chocolate cake – 2.8 ounces – 36 mg

Chocolate brownies – 1.5 ounces – 10 mg

Chocolate mousse – 3.2 ounces – 15 mg

Chocolate pudding – 5.1 ounces – 9 mg

Over-The-Counter Drugs

NoDoz (maximum strength) – 1 tablet – 200 mg

Vivarin – 1 tablet – 200 mg

Excedrin (extra strength) – 2 tablets – 130 mg

Anacin (maximum strength) – 2 tablets – 64 mg

CHAPTER EIGHT

What Happens When You Quit Caffeine?

If you decide to give up caffeine "cold turkey" style, you will feel the impact of withdrawal quite rapidly.

Within 12 to 24 hours after your last cup of coffee or ingestion of caffeine in some form your body will react sufficiently to make you aware that it is looking for its fix. It has become use to functioning one way, but all of a sudden it has to learn to perform another way, but the receptor changes are still in place, waiting for another dose of caffeine.

The universal symptom of caffeine withdrawal is a headache, and it can be quite severe.

Other symptoms of withdrawal include depression, fatigue, lethargy, irritability and even nausea and vomiting.

People often find themselves more short-tempered than usual. If you find yourself shouting in exasperation or blowing your horn repeatedly in heavy traffic, you know that you are experiencing the unpleasant results of withdrawal.

Some people who had been ingesting a lot of caffeine even experience eye muscle spasms.

The first 24 to 48 hours are the worse you are going to feel.

It takes one to two weeks to get over the caffeine withdrawal symptoms, depending on the amount of caffeine you had been taking in and your body type. Most people start to return to normal within about 10 days.

If you are a die-hard coffee drinker, your first question is usually if you will feel as alert and on top of your game if you walk into your office each morning without that familiar caffeine buzz. Will you be as alert, as driven, as energetic?

Yes you will, according to a comprehensive study done by researchers from the University of Vermont College of Medicine and Johns Hopkins School of Medicine.

In the online edition of the scientific journal *Psychopharmacology*, they published their findings of our brain's electrical activity and blood flow during caffeine withdrawal to see what was taking place physiologically during caffeine abstinence with a particular focus on determining the underlying causes of the "caffeine withdrawal headache."

Some of the study participants received caffeine capsules while others received placebo capsules, and all were measured for brain electrical activity, blood flow velocity and personal self-reports on how they were feeling.

The researchers discovered that abruptly stopping caffeine produces changes in cerebral blood flow velocity and quantitative EEG that were believed to be related to the classic caffeine withdrawal symptoms of headache, drowsiness and decreased alertness.

In lay person's terms, when the participants stopped taking in caffeine they had an increased blood flow, and that effect was determined to be the cause of the withdrawal headaches people experience.

Those who quit caffeine also underwent changes in increased theta rhythm (EEG) which explained another common withdrawal symptom of fatigue. The verbal reports from these same study participants listed their feelings of being "tired," "fatigued," "sluggish" and "weary," which was in keeping with the research findings.

But the final conclusion of the study was something the researchers were not expecting to find.

They concluded that there were no net benefits to the body when they were consistently fuelled with caffeine.

Dr. Stacey Sigmon, research associate professor of psychiatry at the University of Vermont and the first author of the study, explained their findings:

"In contrast to what most of us coffee lovers would think, our study showed no difference between when the participant was maintained on chronic placebo and when the participant was stabilized on chronic caffeine administration.

"What this means is that consuming caffeine regularly does not appear to produce any net beneficial effects, based on the measures we examined."

While this is one of the newer studies about the impact of caffeine withdrawal, it has been the focus of medical literature dating back a century. All in all, almost 70 studies on caffeine withdrawal have been published in peer-reviewed medical journals, most of them in the last 15 years.

So how do you stay energized without caffeine? How do you withdraw from your emotional mainstay and not feel a great, dark void of sleepiness and a bad case of the blahs?

According to the Nursing Online Education Centre Database, you heighten your energy level first by getting sufficient sleep at night if you possibly can, and then incorporate some small behavioural changes and tricks that will spurt your energy when you previously reached for a caffeinated beverage.

Here are 10 are their best ideas for bringing energy to your caffeine-free days when you feel you need a boost:

1. Turn on the lights. Your body responds favourably and naturally to changes in light, feeling invigorated by them. So don't work in the natural darkness of a cloudy day; instead turn on a light; it will help you stay alert. Keep your blinds open a bit so the morning sun will stream in and add extra lights to your desk to fight off sleepiness throughout the day.

2. Deal with emotional issues. One of the biggest underlying causes of fatigue and exhaustion is stress. Being upset about parts of your life can sap your energy and make you feel like you need to drink coffee by the bucket. You don't. You have to take the time out to deal with what is troubling you and solve it. Otherwise, not only will it continue to drain you emotionally and physically, but it will cause long term damage to your health and well-being.

3. Exercise. During a recent episode of the new American television series *Elementary*

4. Starring Johnny Lee Miller as Sherlock Holmes and Lucy Liu as Dr. Watson, Holmes starts making coffee to fuel an all-nighter he has to pull to study a mountain of evidence files. Watson shows him her trick of staying awake and creating an instant energy boost with exercise. She does a few jumping jacks, gets her blood moving and presto, she's got the same energy jolt as he gets from a cup of coffee. Funny thing is, though the show is fiction, what she did was fact. Try to work 30 minutes of exercise into your daily schedule. Failing that, when you feel like you are falling asleep and need that caffeine, instead just jump up and do a few jumping jacks and squats. It will give you the same effect.

5. Avoid excess sugar. Don't substitute one bad habit for another. Reaching for a sugary snack when you feel tired will create the same destructive cycle as reaching for caffeine. Sugar causes your energy levels to bottom out once it's been digested, and you will want more in an endless cycle. When you need to be at your peak energy level, avoid sugary foods.

6. Grab a handful of nuts. Keep a secret stash of almonds, cashews, peanuts or walnuts in your desk for a quick energy boost. It really works. Dried fruits and other healthy snacks also work.

7. Get up and move away from your desk. Walk to the washroom or the water fountain or just up and down the hall for a couple of minutes. No matter whether or not you ingest caffeine, you find find hours of sitting at your desk will start to sap your energy. A quick change of scenery and the movement of the walk will restore you.

8. Start your day with your most challenging task. You may think that your brain is in a fog first thing in the morning, but by the time you've showered, dressed, travelled to work and sat down at your desk, it's operating on all cylinders. So keep it in gear by giving it your most difficult job first. Your state of alertness will see you through it and the rest of the day will be a breeze.

9. Have a mint. Keep a little container of peppermints in your desk for when your energy starts to lag. The smell and taste of mint has been found to wake up many people. As an added benefit, your breath will be fresher.

10. Be kind to yourself. Take a few minutes every morning and afternoon to consider your accomplishments for that day, that week, that month and through life in general. There's something about knowing that you are moving emotionally and mentally in the right direction that gives you a secret energy boost. Don't look ahead at the long list of what still has to be done unless you have first thought for a minute at all you have done already. This little mental technique will boost your energy and give you what you need to tackle the next task.

11. Eat sufficient protein. Protein is a vital part of a balanced diet, but is often ignored. If you are not eating sufficient protein, all the caffeine in the world won't keep you from feeling wiped out.

CHAPTER NINE

How To Set Up Your Personal Strategy For Quitting Caffeine

It is common for people who quit caffeine to report within about three months that they feel better and more energetic than they have felt in years. Their energy supply stays steady all day, without the afternoon lags they had grown accustomed to.

They learn that the strangest thing about their coffee drinking habit was that drinking more coffee, while it seemed to give them more energy at the time, actually was counter-productive.

More was not necessarily better, they discover, and science supports this anecdotal evidence.

Studies show that if you drank four cups of coffee at once, that would be about the maximum buzz and feeling of alertness that you could get from it. After that, the effect starts to impact you different.

If you drank 10 cups, for example, you would end up being less alert than if you had ingested no coffee at all.

That's good news when you are trying to quit. Unlike other addictive drugs, caffeine can work its way out of your system and you can completely recover from its withdrawal within about 10 days.

In the grand scheme of life, it beats trying to quit smoking or taking other addictive medications.

A good strategy that has been effective for many coffee drinkers is to first figure out exactly how much caffeine you are taking into your body every week from a variety of sources (coffee, colas, chocolate, medications, etc.) and then make a plan for gradually scaling down over several weeks.

Getting an accurate reading on your intake requires research. Read labels carefully, since caffeine can be found in some foods and medications, not just in coffee, tea and colas.

Map out the intake you will allow yourself, and stick to your plan. Be sure to cut back gradually. For example, eliminate one can of Diet Coke a day over a period of a couple of weeks. Or select a smaller mug for your coffee and start to diminish your intake gradually.

But approaching your withdrawal gradually, you will be able to help your body get used to lower levels of caffeine and diminish the ill effects of withdrawal.

Because you will feel emotionally that you are taking something away from your life, this is also an excellent time to introduce some new and healthful activity into your routine.

Map this new activity into your plan as well. What you need to do is divert your mind from its habit.

For example, you might start a walking program, beginning with shorter, 10 minute walks around your block and working up to a daily hour of brisk walking on a nearby trail. Add a series of deep breathing exercises as well.

Walking and deep breathing are particularly effective companies for your body as you withdraw the caffeine, since both are mind-clearing exercises. Their effect will stay with you and become a new and healthful habit long after your coffee drinking habit is gone.

Start a new hobby that you have long considered. Take up Chinese brush painting or water colours, enter a cooking class, join a non-profit organization that could benefit from your skill set, or try a new craft or project.

The important thing about any new endeavour is that it is something you feel excited about. Enthusiasm breeds energy. If you care deeply about a new activity, it will help you boost your spirits and your energy level.

The hardest cup of coffee to give up is usually the first of the day. Some caffeine-free people found that it worked for them to institute a system of waking themselves up gradually. They set one alarm for 15 minutes earlier than they really needed, and then a second and even a third at five minute intervals.

This slow process of coming awake allowed them to leave their beds in a more alert state than if they had to bolt out at the first loud alarm.

A happy psychological state is also a great energy booster. By adopting an optimistic point of view about life, you will find your energy levels more stable than if you are constantly thinking about the negative implications of things and people around you.

If bad things bring you down, you will feel more worn out than if you put those rose-coloured glasses back on.

Another effective strategy in quitting caffeine is to eat smaller, more frequent meals. If your meals are spaced too far apart, you are allowing your blood glucose to spike and crash, and you will frequently feel tired and hungry throughout your day.

Likewise, if you eat big meals, you will also drag yourself down as your body works hard to digest this sudden and huge intake of food. By levelling out your food intake, you can take a significant step in levelling out the energy peaks and valleys of your day.

If you are still getting that coffee craving in the mid-afternoon, reach for an apple or another fresh fruit instead. Fruits can be digested more easily than many other foods and you will soon feel that all fuelled up buzz again.

Get up in time to have a good breakfast, for that single habit will keep you fuelled all through the morning. Your mother was right; it really is the most important meal of the day.

If your work environment permits it, include aromatherapy as a substitute for pouring a fresh cup of coffee or reaching for a Diet Coke. Smells like citrus, ginger and peppermint give us a feeling of energy and boost our alertness. Light a candle if you can. If that is not possible, try to find a perfume infused with these scent or even a hand cream that you can apply and savour the smell.

Within minutes, you will have the same feeling of energy that you would have accomplished with an ingestion of caffeine.

Sometimes it is helpful to consider that your decision to quit drinking coffee does not mean that you will never have another cup. It means that you will clear out your system.

It does not take away the fact that now that you know what caffeine does to your body, you can still self-administer a cup of coffee in extreme circumstances when you really, really need it. It means that you will recognize caffeine for the drug that it is, not as an emotional crutch or source of comfort or even a mindless part of your social custom.

The social aspect of joining friends for a cup of coffee is one that many users don't want to give up. While you may be willing to make a health change, you do not really want to alter your whole lifestyle.

Most health authorities do not recommend a simple substitution of decaffeinated coffee or tea for regular coffee or tea. That is because decaffeinated coffee still contains about seven milligrams of caffeine per six ounce cup, enough to keep your brain and body dependent on it. Decaffeinated coffee also still has all the acids and oils that can cause problems to your digestive system and your liver.

That can be a major problem. When you consume highly acidic foods and drinks over a period of years, you can strain your body's alkaline balance. The body then tries to neutralize the acids and uses calcium as a buffering agent.

The issue is that coffee uses up your available calcium and pushes you to excrete any excess calcium in your urine. This further depletes your calcium supply and leaves you susceptible to osteoporosis which affects the bone health of men and women.

An effective approach is to start mixing your normal cup of coffee with ¼ to ¾ cup of herbal coffee. Gradually reduce the percentage of your regular caffeine-laced coffee over a two to three week period until you are drinking only the herbal coffee.

This approach can be very effective in reducing withdrawal headaches and helping your body gradually reduce its dependence on the stimulant.

Herbal coffee is particularly versatile. It can be brewed in drip coffee makers, percolators, and espresso machines and it comes in a variety of flavors.

You can also shorten the brew time or expose yourself to a wide variety of herbal teas on the market. The shorter brewing time, the less caffeine in a cup of tea.

When it comes to treating your caffeine withdrawal symptoms, be careful about what kind of headache remedies you reach for. Many over-the-counter pain relievers contain caffeine, so while they will temporarily ease your headache, it will just return with a vengeance the next day. Look for caffeine-free pain relievers.

Remember to drink more water when you are eliminating caffeine from your daily diet. Try to drink at least eight cups a day during the withdrawal process.

If the feeling of fatigue is overwhelming, you can consider taking a nutritional supplement with B vitamins and pantothenic acid (B-5). What you will be doing is increasing your metabolic efficiency, which will give you the same feeling but will not be as habit forming as stimulating your nervous system with caffeine.

If you are experiencing digestive issues from the withdrawal of caffeine, add a refreshing aloe vera juice to your diet. Its anti-bacterial components will help soothe the discomfort you are experiencing.

The important thing is to take it one day at a time. No life change occurs without consequences, and quitting caffeine is a major life change. Give yourself time to make it happen and don't give up.

If you do all of these things and are still fighting a deep, overwhelming feeling of fatigue, schedule a physical with your doctor. There are many illnesses, some serious and some minor, that can sap your energy and give you a feeling of chronic sluggishness. You may be fighting mono, an underactive thyroid, or anemia. Get yourself checked out.

CHAPTER TEN

Substitutions For Your Cups of Coffee

Once you put your mind to eliminating caffeine from your diet, you start looking for coffee alternatives. Unlike other things you may quit in life, this single withdrawal from a cup of a hot beverage signals a lifestyle change that most of us don't want.

We don't want to walk away from the coffee area at work because we will feel excluded from the camaraderie and gossip.

We don't want to give up the pleasure of wrapping our cold hands around a cup of hot, soothing comfort.

So we start to look for substitutions.

One of the simplest ways to reduce your caffeine intake is to switch from drinking coffee to tea. While both green and black teas contain caffeine, it is considerably less. As well, green tea has a health balance because it is filled with anti-oxidants which have been connected with weight loss by increasing fat oxidation.

Rooibos tea, also called red tea, is another viable substitute for coffee. Made popular in South Africa, it is now in supermarkets across North America and Europe. Organic rooibos tea is caffeine free and so naturally sweet that it is mainly consumed without either milk or sugar.

Teeccino is a brand of herbal coffee that is all-herbal and completely caffeine free. With the same robust flavour associated with regular coffee, it is instead a mixture of grains, fruits and nuts. The original formula consisted of carob, chicory, dates, figs and almonds. Ramon nuts, which have a flavour similar to coffee, were added later to the recipe. This drink is prepared by brewing it in a coffee maker or espresso machine.

Another excellent substitute for coffee is yerba mate, a tea-like beverage that contains no caffeine at all. Extremely popular in Argentina and other South American countries, it is sipped from a small wood cup with a straw that sifts the liquid that has absorbed the flavor from the mate leaves.

Roastaroma, packaged as an herbal tea bag, is comprised of grains and spices that give it a coffee-like taste, yet it contains no caffeine. Instead, it is a mixture of roasted barley, roasted chicory, roasted carob, cinnamon, allspice and Chinese star anise.

A common coffee substitute in Europe is Bambu, an instant drink that is comprised of chicory, figs, wheat, acorns and malted barley. It has been around for about 50 years, but has been growing in favour in recent years.

In Australia, people looking for a comforting hot beverage without caffeine are turning to Soyafe, a caffeine-free blend of roasted soy beans with the natural sweetener, Stevia. Like Bambu, it comes in a powdered form like instant coffee with only boiling hot water needed to bring out its taste.

Other coffee substitutes are Pero, Grain Gourmet and Inka Naturalis which all contain different blends of barley, rye, and chicory. Grain Gourmet has barley malt, while Inka has beet roots.

A common ingredient in most coffee substitutes is chicory, which carries the same rich flavour but has been cited for its health benefits. These include purifying your blood and aiding your liver function.

Whatever substitution you use, you will find that ultimately it gives you the same comforting feeling as nursing a hot cup of coffee, without the serious impact on your body systems.

The key is to find warm and nourishing replacements that work for you.

When you eliminate caffeine from your daily routine, you can look forward to enjoying all its social benefits without upsetting your body and creating addictive behaviour patterns.

In the long run, you will feel more energized and healthier than ever before. Plus, there will be no long lineups before you start your day feeling good.

www.ingramcontent.com/pod-product-compliance
Lightning Source LLC
Chambersburg PA
CBHW041214270326
41930CB00001B/18